In Remembrance of the
Olympic Games 1908
J B Davidson

A Guide to London 1908 - In Remembrance of the Olympic Games 1908
Mapseeker Archive Publishing Ltd.

First published 2012

Copyright © Mapseeker Archive Publishing Ltd, 2012

Text © Paul Leslie Line

Maps and photographs © as per credits on page 144

Printed in the West Midlands.

British Library Cataloguing in publication data.
A catalogue record for this book is available from the British Library.

ISBN 978 1 84491 787 7

Typesetting and origination by Mapseeker Archive Publishing.

Historical maps available to view and buy at
www.mapseeker.co.uk

IN REMEMBRANCE OF THE OLYMPIC GAMES 1908

A GUIDE TO LONDON 1908

IN REMEMBRANCE OF THE OLYMPIC GAMES 1908

MAPSEEKER ARCHIVE PUBLISHING

FOREWORD BY KATE HOEY M.P.

COLLINS BARTHOLOMEW

COLLINS BARTHOLOMEW
HISTORIC MAP ARCHIVE

MAPSEEKER
ARCHIVE PUBLISHING
GATEWAY TO OUR HISTORIC PAST
www.mapseeker.co.uk

FOREWORD

No doubt we will expect to see vast numbers of commemorative books in this the year of the London Olympics, but I would be amazed to come across another that is so clearly a labour of love. To be able to place ourselves so thoroughly in the London of that other Olympic year, 1908, and to explore the reassuring patterns of the streets, helps us recognise on one hand the continuity and on the other the change to London since then.

Each of the detailed street maps is a treasure - including showing the "omnibus and tramway routes" - but, of particular delight to me, is the one on page 70, showing South London, including my constituency of Vauxhall. Anyone reading this treasure trove of history will want to see what their area looked like over a hundred years ago and it is all beautifully laid out.

Some things never change, even 104 years later. What shines through is the dedication of the athletes and of all the volunteers who made the Games possible. 1908 may have been the pinnacle of amateurism as an ideal, and the competitors' enthusiasm, as well as their genuine focus, is clear in each photograph. However, even then the invaluable letters and documents that detail the organisation of the events demonstrate that this was demanding and tireless work – despite no television audience of billions!

The instructions to participants in the marathon are particularly interesting and show that even then sponsorship was crucial. The OXO Company was appointed the official caters and there is the list of all that was to be supplied free to the competitors, including eau de cologne and bananas. In 1908, five hotels were named as accommodation for the runners to have a "wash, etc: en route" - something Paula Radcliffe probably wished for in the 2005 London Marathon.

Some might think that drugs are a new problem, but in 1908 Rule 4 stated firmly that "no competitor either at the start or during the progress of the race may take or receive any drug. The breach of this rule will operate as an absolute disqualification."

As the former Sports Minister I experienced the Sydney Olympic Games directly in 2000. For anyone who loves sport, the Olympics are the absolute pinnacle of sporting achievement. We owe so much to the early pioneers and this little gem of a book will make sure that the 1908 Games can be recognised in their proper historic setting.

I have no doubt whatsoever that this book would make a treasured gift to every member of the International Olympic Committee when they arrive this summer.

Kate Hoey M.P. for Vauxhall, London.
Sports Minister 1999-2001

Early 19th century view - The Old Village of Vauxhall, South London, with entrance to the gardens.

ACKNOWLEDGEMENTS

Many people have contributed in producing this commemorative book, A Guide to London 1908 in Remembrance of the 1908 Olympics. I would like to express my grateful thanks and acknowledgments to everyone who has played a part, however small, in creating a historic tribute to the early pioneers of the great games and the legacy that they bestowed on many generations throughout the World.

Sheena Barclay MD, Kathryn Kelly, Jethro Lennox and the rest of the team at Harper Collins, Glasgow, for their continued support, and the sourcing of the antique original Atlas and Guide to London 1908 from the Collins Bartholomew Map Archive.

Sue Worrell and Martin Killeen, the Cadbury Research Library, Special Collections - Academic Services – The University of Birmingham in the sourcing of the William Barnard collection of memorabilia from the 1908 London Olympics.

Elaine Penn, Anna Mcnally and Claire Brunnen, The University of Westminster Archive Services for the sourcing of the original plan of the route of the London 1908 Olympic Marathon, portrait image of William Barnard and their contribution to archive research.

Adrian Whitter, Avante Visual Communications, for his creative illustrative work in the design and compilation of the book.

Helen Clare Cromarty, Executive Committee Member of the Wenlock Olympian Society for her contribution to "The Rise of Olympism".

Tom McCook, President of Birchfield Harriers, Birmingham, and Karen Woodcock, Marketing Consultant, for their valuable support in the final stages of the book's publication.

Matthew Langham for his editorial work for the book, especially The 1908 London Olympic Marathon.

Steve Toulouse, Senior Graphic Artist, Mapseeker Publishing, who has contributed many hours over the last two years in the preparation of the original archives that have been recreated for everyone to appreciate in this commemorative publication.

Paul Leslie Line, Mapseeker Publishing Ltd.

The Great Stadium, London 1908.

INTRODUCTION

The Atlas and Guide to the London Olympics of 1908, now re-published with kind permission of Collins Bartholomew, acts as both an archival accolade of Edwardian London and a tribute to the visionaries who, unknowingly at the time, ignited a flame that would continue to burn into the next millennium, uniting nations in sport.

The guide began humbly as a simple, unassuming scrapbook compiled by William Barnard which eventually came to be stored in the archives of Birmingham University, having been generously donated by the British Amateur Athletics Association (AAA). Barnard, Honorary Secretary for the Polytechnic Harriers who organised the 1908 Olympic marathon, was appointed as official timekeeper for the 1908 Olympic Games at very short notice and subsequently served as the AAA's Honorary Treasurer from 1910 until 1932.

Following his experience of the ground-breaking London Olympics of 1908, Barnard began to assemble what was to become a treasured collection of personal mementoes and artefacts, the first of which was a signed portrait picture of fellow official I. B. Davidson. The title of this book is in fact taken from Davidson's addition of "In Remembrance of the 1908 Olympics" along with his signature on the photograph. His official role of Motor and Attendants' Marshal was also as unique as it was interesting. During the historic 1908 London Olympic marathon, one famed for its epic finish, early motor cars donated by companies including Wolseley and Napier made their major sporting debut, carrying race officials, following runners along the course and picking up those unable to continue.

The centrepiece to William Barnard's scrapbook, also reproduced in this book, are the original, illuminating letters of appeal compiled by Lord Desborough of Taplow, President of the British Olympic Council, who was canvassing for the financial support needed for London to successfully host the Olympics. Despite the substantial obstacles of having just 10 months to find a suitable venue, build a bespoke stadium and secure the necessary finance, he nonetheless campaigned vigorously. With Desborough's influence – he was a consummate organiser and inspirational figurehead - all the finances were secured with just two weeks to the deadline, further aided when Lord Northcliffe, proprietor of the Daily Mail, agreed to sponsor the games and support appeals for funding via his newspaper.

With the event secured, the London games of 1908 would go on to be globally significant, with the introduction of national teams, a parade at a dedicated opening ceremony, winners' medals and the construction of first–class sporting facilities chief among its innovations. The official programmes for the Olympics, a rich source of illuminating contemporary information, are also reproduced here.

Travel at the time was, for many people, made possible by the large and well established railway network, with some totally reliant upon it. In the capital, the London Underground enabled visitors to explore the many sights and places of interest in the City of London with affordability and ease. As the crowds thronged to the Olympics of 1908, a new notion of tourism was fast becoming fashionable and widespread, with its advent also in step with an increasing number of people owning a motor car, not just the privileged few. John Bartholomew, fifth in a family line of famous cartographers, saw the commercial potential in this growing leisure travel market, and began producing handy pocket sized atlases for use in navigating the rapidly expanding road network and locating London's many attractions. Much of the information from such a typical guide is republished here, giving real day-to-day insight into the mechanics of hosting the Olympics and the nature of travel at the time.

After the ground-breaking games of 1908, operating under an ethos of continuous improvement and fairness, the International Olympics Committee introduced unified rules that included lanes in running events, and a requirement that officials originate from more than one country. As such, the 1908 London Olympics both reinvigorated and established the blueprint for the modern games, transforming the Olympics into the global sporting event we recognise today that is embraced the world over. It is hoped in that reproducing many contemporary documents from 1908 its legacy can be similarly refreshed and its rich history brought to life through this book.

Paul Leslie Line
Mapseeker Archive Publishing

AMATEUR ATHLETIC ASSOCIATION.

ESTABLISHED 1880

TELEGRAPHIC ADDRESS,
"ATHLETE, LONDON"

TELEPHONE:
CITY, 902.

Office.— 10, John Street, Adelphi, W.C.

Office Hours—11 to 5.   Saturdays, 11 to 1.

June 15, 1908.

DEAR SIR,

I have the pleasure to inform you that you have been appointed to act in the official capacity of a *Time Keeper for Marathon Race* at the Olympic Games, on the following dates, viz.:

July 24 ————————————

and I shall be glad if you will please let me know by return, whether your services will be available on those dates. As only the absolute necessary number of Officials have been appointed for each day, it is essential those definitely accepting are certain to officiate.

As a full list of Officials has to be supplied to the British Olympic Council by Friday, the 19th inst., I would ask for your immediate reply.

I believe the Games will commence at 10 o'clock in the morning, until 1 o'clock, and then continue from 2.30 to 6.30.

Yours faithfully,

P. L. FISHER,

Hon. Sec.

Wm Barua

CONTENTS

CONTENTS

Panoramic view of the Great Stadium, Olympic Games London 1908.

Forrest Smithson from the USA, winner of the 110m hurdles event, running with a Bible in his hand.

One

GUIDE AND GAZETTEER
OF LONDON 1908

AREA AND POPULATION, 1901.

	Area in Sq. Miles.	Population.
London, within the Registrar-General's Tables of Mortality	116¼	4,536,541
Administrative County of London	116¼	4,536,541
London School Board District	116¼	4,536,541
Metropolitan Parliamentary Boroughs	116¼	4,519,838
The "Greater London" of the Registrar-General's Weekly Return ..	693	6,581,372
Consisting of—		
(a) Metropolitan Police District	692	6,554,449
(b) City of London, within the Municipal and Parliamentary limits	1	26,923

The figures for the City represent the *night* population; during the business hours of the day it rises to over 1,000,000.

The population of London in 1801 was 958,863; in 1811, 1,138.815; in 1821, 1,378,947; in 1831, 1,654,994; in 1841, 1,948,369; in 1851, 2,362.236; in 1861, 2,803,989; in 1871, 3,254,260; in 1881, 3,816,483; in 1891, 4,231,431.

Parliamentary—London is divided into 28 electoral divisions, and returns 61 members to the House of Commons. London University also returns a member.

Under the Local Government (England and Wales) Act, 1888, London is an administrative county, which returns a total of 118 members to the County Council. By the Act of 1899, which came into force on November 1, 1900, the County of London, exclusive of the City, is divided into 28 boroughs, each with a mayor, alderman, and councillors. These borough councils practically take over the powers and duties of the old parish vestries.

Chronology.—London destroyed by Boadicea, A.D. 61; rebuilt by Theodosius about 306; ravaged by plague, 644; burnt, 798 and 801; made the capital by King Alfred, 893; made a mint town by Athelstane in 925; burnt, 1077, and again in 1136; first mayor appointed, 1190; wasted by plague, 1349 and 1369; scene of Wat Tyler's rebellion, 1381; first lighted by lanterns, 1416; scene of Jack Cade's rebellion, 1450; also date of first lord mayor's show; visited by plague, 1500, 1525, and 1548; houses first built of brick, 1470; Lady Jane Grey appeared in the city, 1553; visited by Elizabeth, 1570; by James I. in 1603; first newspaper published, 1622; first hackney coach appeared, 1634; coal first used, 1640; Charles I. beheaded at Whitehall, 1649; visited by Cromwell, 1651; ravaged by great plague, 1664-66; nearly destroyed by fire, 1666; G.P.O. established, 1711; Gordon riots took place, 1780; first canal opened, 1801; cabs first in use, 1820; New London Bridge opened, 1831; first Great World's Exhibition held, 1851; great fire in Tooley Street, 1861; second great Exhibition, 1862; great explosion of gunpowder in Erith Marshes, 1864; Queen's Jubilee, 1887; **Tower Bridge opened, 1894;** Queen's Diamond Jubilee celebrations, 1897; funeral of Queen Victoria, 1901; Coronation of King Edward VII., 1902.

POPULATION OF METROPOLITAN BOROUGHS.

Battersea	168,907	Kensington	176,628
Bermondsey	130,760	Lambeth	301,895
Bethnal Green	129,680	Lewisham	127,495
Camberwell	259,339	Paddington	143,976
Chelsea	73,842	Poplar	168,822
City of London..	26,923	St. Marylebone	133,301
Deptford	110,398	St. Pancras	235,317
Finsbury	101,463	Shoreditch	118,637
Fulham	137,289	Southwark	206,180
Greenwich	95,770	Stepney	298,000
Hackney	219,272	Stoke Newington	51,247
Hammersmith	112,239	Wandsworth	232,034
Hampstead	81,942	Westminster	183,011
Holborn	59,405	Woolwich	117,178
Islington	334,991		

ALPHABETICAL GUIDE AND GAZETTEER

To Places of Interest and Amusement in

LONDON AND ITS ENVIRONS

The Figures and Index Letters refer to the location of places in the Maps in the Atlas.

Plate No.

Abbey Wood, near Erith, Kent. 11½ m. by S.E. and C. Ry. from Charing Cross or Cannon Street .. .. Cb 5

Abney Park Cemetery, Stoke Newington .. .. Ba 9

Academy, Royal, Burlington House, Piccadilly. Exhibitions of Paintings, May to July. Admission, 1s.; evening, 6d. .. .. .. Bb 7

Achilles Monument, It was subscribed for by English ladies, and cast from cannon taken in the Peninsular War and at Waterloo .. Ac 7

Adelphi Theatre, 411 Strand .. .. Cb 7

Admiralty. The offices are in Whitehall. Hours, 10-5 .. .. Cc 7

Agnew's New Art Gallery, Old Bond St. 1s., including Catalogue .. Bb 7

Agricultural Hall, Islington. Christmas cattle shows, military tournaments, etc. .. .. Dc 10

Albert Embankment, opened in 1869, cost over £1,000,000 .. .. Dd 7

Albert Hall, South Kensington. Seats 8000 people. Has a splendid organ. Sunday Concerts a speciality .. .. Cc 11

Albert Memorial, Kensington Gardens. Erected to the memory of the late Prince Consort, and designed by Sir J. Gilbert Scott. Cost £120,000 .. Cc 11

Albert Suspension Bridge, Chelsea to Battersea Park. Opened 1873 Cb 12

Aldwych Theatre, Aldwych .. .. Db 7

Alexandra House, west side of Albert Hall. A home for female students Cc 11

Alexandra Palace, Muswell Hill. Open 10 a.m. to 9 p.m., free .. Ca 4

Alexandra Theatre, Stoke Newington Road .. .. .. Cb 9

Alhambra Theatre of Varieties, Leicester Sq. Ballets a special feature Cb 7

Allan Wesleyan Library, City Road. Contains fine collection of Biblical and Theological works .. .. Bd 9

Alexandra Hospital, for Children with hip disease, Queen Sq., Bloomsbury Cb 8

All Hallows, Barking Church, Gt. Tower Street .. .. .. Cc 6

All Hallows Church, Orange Street, Leicester Square .. .. Cb 7

All Saints' Church, Margaret Street, by Butterfield; lavishly decorated Bc 8

American Reading Rooms, Gilligs' U.S. Exchange, 9 Strand .. Cb 7

Anglo-American Exchange, 3 Northumberland Avenue .. .. Cb 7

Antiquarian Society's Museum, Burlington House. Daily, 10-4; Saturdays, 10-2; closed in September. On application to the Secretary .. Bb 7

Apollo Theatre, Shaftesbury Avenue .. .. Bb 7

Apothecaries' Hall, Water Lane, Blackfriars .. .. .. Ac 6

Apsley House, Hyde Park Corner. Residence of the Duke of Wellington Ac 7

Archæological Institute, Royal, Hanover Square .. .. .. Ba 7

Architectural Museum, 18 Tufton Street, Dean's Yard, Westminster. Open daily, free, from 10-4; Saturdays, to 8 p.m. .. .. .. Cd 7

Armourers' Hall, Coleman Street. Collection of Arms, etc. Daily .. Bb 6

Art Training Schools, South Kensington; for Art training of male and female students .. .. Cd 11

Arts, Society of, John Street, Adelphi. Open free daily, from 10-4, except on Wednesdays and Saturdays .. .. Cb 7

Ascot. Celebrated for its races in June. By L. & S.W. to Ascot, or by Windsor, G.W. and drive along Queen Anne's Ride .. .. .. Ac 18

Avenue Theatre, Northumberland Avenue, rebuilt as the PLAYHOUSE Cb 7

Baltic Chambers, St Mary Axe .. .. Cb 6

Band of Hope Jubilee Building, Old Bailey .. .. .. Ab 6

Bank of England, Threadneedle Street. Public rooms, daily, 10-4; Saturdays, 10-2. Vaults, etc., by order of a Director .. .. .. Bb 6

M. Schilles and A. Auffray of France, winners of the gold medal in the 2000 metre tandem race.

Plate No.

Bankers' Clearing House, Lombard Street .. .. Bc 6
Banstead Downs, Surrey, 16 m. by L., B., & S. C. Ry. .. .. Dc 18
Baptist College, Regent's Park .. .. Bc 10
Barbers' Hall, Cripplegate. Designed by Inigo Jones .. .. Bb 6
Barking, Essex, 7½ m. by Gt. E. Ry. from Fenchurch St. or N.
    London Ry. .. .. Cb 5
Barnard's Inn, Holborn ; was one of the Inns of Chancery, now one of
    the Mercers' Company's Schools .. .. Dc 8
Barnardo's Homes for Destitute Children, Commercial Road .. Ab 14
Barnet, 10 m. by Gt. N. Ry. from King's Cross .. .. .. Ba 5
Battersea Bridge, between Chelsea and Battersea. Opened in 1891 .. Cb 12
Battersea Park, about 200 acres in extent. Laid out in 1852-58. The
    sub-tropical garden is a special feature .. .. .. Db 12
Battersea Polytechnic Institute, includes workshops, laboratories, art
    and music rooms. Organ recitals .. .. Db 12
Bechstein Hall, Wigmore Street. Concerts, etc. .. .. .. Ac 8
Bedford College, York Place. A University College for women .. Db 11
Bedford Music Hall, High Street, Camden Town .. .. .. Cc 10
Belgrave Hospital, Clapham Road, for children .. .. .. Bc 13
Bermondsey Market, for hides and leather, Bermondsey, S.E. .. Ca 13
Bethlehem Hospital, for lunatics, Lambeth Road, S.E. .. .. Ed 7
Bethnal Green Infirmary, Cambridge Road .. .. .. Cc 9
Bethnal Green Museum, near Victoria Park. Free daily. Mondays,
    Thursdays, and Saturdays, 10 a.m. to 10 p.m. ; Tuesdays, Wednesdays,
    and Fridays, 10 a.m. to 4, 5, or 6 p.m., according to season ; Sundays
    from 2 p.m. till dusk .. .. Cc 9
Bexley, 13½ m. by S. E. and C. Ry. from Charing Cross or Cannon Street Cb 5
Big Ben, the name of the bell in the Clock Tower of the Houses of Parliament Cc 7
Billingsgate, Thames Street, is the wholesale fish market of London .. Cc 6
Bishopsgate Institute, Library, Reading Rooms, etc. .. .. Cb 6
Bisley, 28 m. by L. and S.W. Ry. from Waterloo. Annual Meeting of
    National Rifle Association .. .. Ac 5
Blackfriars Bridge. Opened by Queen Victoria in 1869 .. .. Ac 6
Blackheath, near Greenwich, 267 acres in extent. By S.E. and C. Ry.
    Here Wat Tyler in 1381, and Jack Cade in 1450, assembled the rebel-
    lious "men of Kent," who were bent on attacking the Metropolis .. Db 4
Blackwall Basin, West India Docks. Area, 6¾ acres .. .. Cc 14
Blackwall Tunnel, between Poplar and Greenwich. Opened in 1897 .. Dc 14
Bloomsbury County Court, Great Portland Street .. .. .. Ab 8
Board of Agriculture, 4 Whitehall Place, and 3 St James' Sq. Hours 10 to 5 Cc 7
Board of Trade, 7 Whitehall Gardens. Hours 11 to 5 .. .. Cc 7
Borough Market, Southwark. Fruit and Vegetables .. .. Bb 13
Borough Theatre, High Street, Stratford .. ..
Botanic Gardens, Kew. Open free on week days from 10 till dusk ;
    Sunday afternoons from 1 o'clock .. .. Ba 17
Botanic Gardens, Regent's Park. Admission, Mondays and Saturdays,
    1/- ; other days, by order from a Fellow .. .. .. Ab 8
Bow Street Police Court. The most important in London. .. .. Cb 7
Box Hill. Stations on the Brighton, and S.E. Railways. A great holiday
    resort. *The Deepdene,* a house full of art treasures, with beautiful
    grounds, lying east of Dorking, may be visited at the same time. Box
    Hill may also be approached from Betchworth, walking *via* Brockham Bc 5
Brasted and Brasted Park, Kent, 20 miles by rail from London Bridge Cc 5
Bricket Wood, Herts., 3½ m. from St Albans. By rail from Euston .. Ba 5
Bridgewater House, Cleveland Row, contains fine collection of pictures.
    Admission to picture hall on Wednesdays and Saturdays by recommend-
    ation .. .. Bc 7
British and Foreign Bible Society, 146 Queen Victoria Street .. Ac 6
British Association, for the advancement of Science. Office at Burling-
    ton House .. .. Bb 7
British College (late Birkbeck Institution), Breams Buildings .. .. Dc 8

Plate No.

British Museum, free. The hours of admission are from 10 all the year
  round; in January, February, November, December, till 4; March,
  April, September, October, till 5; and May to August, till 6. On
  Monday and Saturday, from May 1st to the middle of July, till 8; and
  onwards to the end of August till 7. The Reading Room is open daily
  from 9, September to April inclusive, till 8; and May to August, till 7.
  Readers must be recommended by a householder. .. .. .. **Cc 8**

British Museum of Natural History. The departments of Zoology,
  Botany, Geology, and Mineralogy are now in Cromwell Road, South
  Kensington. Open from 10 till dusk. On Mondays and Saturdays, May
  1st to July 15th, open till 8, and July 16th to August 31st, till 7.
  Free.   Also on Sundays, 2 or 2.30 till 7 p.m. .. .. .. **Cd 11**

Britannia Theatre, 117 Hoxton Street .. .. **Bc 9**

Brixton Theatre, Brixton Oval .. .. **Bc 13**

Broadway Theatre, New Cross Road .. .. **Ce 14**

Brockwell Park, Herne Hill, 127 acres in extent, opened in 1892 .. **Bb 16**

Bromley, Kent, 12½ m. by S.E. and Chatham Railway .. .. **Bb 5**

Brompton Cemetery, lies between Richmond Road and Fulham Road **Ba 12**

Brompton Oratory, Roman Catholic Church, remarkable for interior
  decorations .. .. **Cd 11**

Broxbourne, Herts., by rail from Liverpool Street and St Pancras .. **Ba 5**

Buckhurst Hill, 10 m. by Gt. Eastern Railway. .. .. .. **Ba 5**

Buckingham Palace, St James's Park.—London residence of the King
  and Queen. Admission to the Royal Stables may be obtained by an
  order from the Master of the Horse .. .. **Bc 7**

Bunhill Fields, Finsbury. Burial place of John Bunyan, Daniel Defoe,
  Dr Isaac Watts .. .. **Ba 6**

Burlington Arcade, Piccadilly .. .. **Bb 7**

Burlington House, Piccadilly. The Royal Academy, Royal Society, and
  other learned Societies are housed here .. .. **Bb 7**

Burnham Beeches.—Now secured as a public resort by the Corporation
  of London. By rail from Paddington to Slough, whence omnibus (1/6).
  Or from Burnham Beeches station by a 40 min. walk. The Beeches are
  the finest in England, their autumn colours being magnificent. .. **Aa 18**

Bushy House, Teddington. A National Physical Laboratory was opened
  in 1902. Kew Observatory is a department of this establishment .. **Ac 17**

Bushy Park. With famous chestnut avenue, is a royal domain of 1000
  acres. Hampton Court or Teddington Stations. .. .. .. **Ac 17**

Camberwell Cemetery, near Honor Oak Station, S.E. and Chatham Ry. **Cb 16**

Cambridge Music Hall, Commercial Street .. .. **Db 6**

Camden Technical Institute, Lancaster Road, Notting Hill .. .. **Bb 11**

Camden Theatre, Crowndale Road .. .. **Ba 8**

Cancer Hospital, Fulham Road, Brompton .. .. **Ca 12**

Canonbury Tower, Canonbury Square.—A relic of the country residence
  of the Priors of St Bartholomew .. .. **Bb 9**

Canterbury Music Hall, Westminster Bridge Road .. .. .. **Dd 7**

Carlyle's House, No. 24 Cheyne Row, Chelsea.—Residence of Thomas
  Carlyle from 1834 to 1881. Open from 10 a.m. till sunset, 1/; Saturdays, 6d. .. .. **Cb 12**

Catford Bridge.—Stations on the S. E. and C. Ry. Occasional county
  cricket matches .. .. **Db 18**

Catholic Apostolic Church, Gordon Square .. .. **Cb 8**

Central Criminal Court, Old Bailey .. .. **Ab 6**

Central Jewish Synagogue, Gt. Portland Street .. .. .. **Bc 8**

Chalfont St Giles.—See Rickmansworth.

Chapel Royal, Savoy Street, Strand. Built between 1505 and 1511, on the
  site of the old Savoy Palace .. .. **Db 7**

Chapel Royal, St James's. Services at 10, 12, and 5.30. Tickets from
  the Lord Chamberlain .. .. **Bc 7**

Chapel Royal, Whitehall. Museum of the Royal United Service Institution, for National treasures connected with Army and Navy; daily, 6d. **Cc 7**

		Plate No.

Charing Cross.—Derives its name from the village of Cherringe, which stood here in the 13th cent. Here Edward I. erected a cross as a memorial to his Queen .. .. Cb 7

Charing Cross Hospital, Agar Street .. .. .. Cb 7

Charing Cross Railway Bridge, on one side of which is a footway. .. Dc 7

Charlton Pier.—The training ship "Warspite," lies off here .. .. Cb 15

Charterhouse, Smithfield.—Once a Carthusian monastery, founded in 1371. In 1611 it was purchased by Thomas Sutton as a school for 40 poor boys and a home for 80 poor men. In 1872 the school was transferred to Godalming, in Surrey. The building is now used as a school for the Merchant Taylors' Company .. .. Aa 6

Chelsea Barracks, Chelsea Bridge Road .. .. .. Da 12

Chelsea Embankment.—Between the Albert and Victoria Bridges .. Da 12

Chelsea Hospital.—An institution for old and invalid soldiers, founded in the reign of Charles II., the building being designed by Sir Christopher Wren. The gardens are open daily, free. Visitors may attend the Sunday Services in the Chapel .. .. Da 12

Chelsea Old Church.—A very interesting old church. Reminiscences of Sir Thomas More, who was probably buried here .. .. Cb 12

Chelsea Palace Variety Theatre, King's Road .. .. Ca 12

Chenies.—2¾ m. from Chorley Wood sta. The *Mortuary Chapel* contains the tombs of the Russell family from the year 1556 (admission orders at the Bedford Estate Office, Montague Street, Russell Square). Chenies is an extremely picturesque spot, and six miles' walk or wheeling along the Chess, passing *Latimers* (Lord Chesham), will bring the tourist to Chesham, 4½ m. from Amersham .. .. Aa 5

Cheshunt, Herts. 17 m. by Gt. N. Ry. Cheshunt Gt. House and Cromwell relics; also *Temple Bar* re-erected at entrance to Theobald's Park .. Ba 5

Cheyne Hospital, for children, Cheyne Walk .. .. .. Cb 12

Chislehurst, Kent. Napoleon III. died here in exile, January 3rd 1873. 11 m. by S.E. and C. Ry., from London Bridge .. .. Cb 5

Chiswick. 8½ m. by S.W. Ry., from Waterloo, or from Ludgate Hill .. Ba 17

Christ Church, Lancaster Gate .. .. Cc 11

Christ Church (Congregational), Wesminster Bridge Road .. .. Dd 7

Christ's Hospital, Newgate Street. The Scholars were removed in April 1902, to new school erected at Horsham, Sussex .. .. Ab 6

City of London Cemetery, Manor Park Station, from Liverpool Street Da 4

City of London Chess Club, Grocers' Hall Court, Poultry .. Bc 6

City of London College, White Street, Moorfields .. .. Bb 6

City of London School, Thames Embankment. Established by the City Corporation in 1834 .. .. Eb 7

City Temple, Holborn Viaduct. Services at 11 a.m., and 7 p.m. .. Ec 8

City and Guilds of London Institute (Gresham College). For the management of technical education in London .. .. Bb 6

City Museum, Guildhall.—Antiquities, etc., daily, 10-4 or 5 .. Bb 6

City of London Consumption Hosp., Approach Rd., Bethnal Green .. Dc 9

City Road Wesleyan Chapel, where John Wesley preached .. Bd 9

Clapham Common, 220 acres, by tramway from Blackfriars or Westminster Bridge; or by City and S. London Ry. to Clapham Common Station .. Bb 16

Clare Market, Strand. Near here is the site of the ancient palace of John, Earl of Clare, 1617 .. .. Da 7

Clarence House, on W. side of St James' Palace, is a Royal residence .. Bc 7

Clement's Inn, Strand, one of the Inns of Chancery .. .. Dc 8

Cleopatra's Needle, Victoria Embankment, an Egyptian obelisk erected in 1878, 168 feet in height .. .. Db 7

Clifford's Inn, Fleet Street, one of the Inns of Chancery .. .. Dc 8

Clissold Park, Stoke Newington, 55 acres in extent, and opened in 1889 Ba 9

Clothworkers' Hall, Mincing Lane, Fenchurch Street .. .. Cc 6

Coal Exchange, Lower Thames Street. Busiest time on Monday, Wednesday, and Friday about 1 p.m. The Roman Bath is shown on Tuesday, Thursday, and Saturday, 12-2; gratuity .. .. Cc 6

A Great Leap for Womankind (Lady doing the "standing" high jump).

	Plate	No.
Cobham Hall, 4 m. S. of Gravesend. Seat of Earl of Darnley. Magnificent park and fine collection of pictures. Open on Fridays (11 to 4) ..	Cb	5
Coliseum, St Martin's Lane	Cb	7
Collins's Music Hall, Islington Green, N.	Ac	9
Colonial Institute, Northumberland Avenue, provides a meeting place for gentlemen connected with the British Colonies and India	Cb	7
Colonial Office, Whitehall, where all state business connected with the British Colonies is conducted by the Colonial Secretary	Cc	7
Columbia Market, Bethnal Green, for the sale of fish	Cd	9
Comedy Theatre, Panton Street, Haymarket	Cb	7
Commissionaires, in green uniform, convey messages, etc., and can be trusted. The charge is 3d. a mile, or 6d. an hour. Office, 419 Strand ..	Cb	7
Congregational Memorial Hall, Farringdon Street	Ec	8
Consumption Hospital, Fulham Road	Ca	12
Cookham, 27½ m. by G.W.Ry., a popular place with London excursionists	Ab	5
Cooper's Hill, near Egham, Surrey, with the Royal Indian Engineering College, established 1870. The College was closed in 1906	Bb	18
Corn Exchange, Mark Lane. Market days, Monday, Wednesday, and Friday, 11-3	Cc	6
Coronet Theatre, High Street, Notting Hill	Bc	11
Corporation Art Gallery, Guildhall, daily, 10 to 4 or 5, free	Bb	6
Court Theatre, Sloane Square, Chelsea	Da	12
Covent Garden Market, for the sale of vegetables, fruit, and flowers. Market days, Tuesday, Thursday, and Saturday, but fruit and flowers are on sale every day	Cb	7
Covent Garden Theatre (Royal Italian Opera), Bow Street	Cb	7
Criterion Theatre, Piccadilly Circus	Bb	7
Crosby Hall, Bishopsgate Street. Built in 1466, afterwards occupied by Richard III. and Sir Thomas More. Now a restaurant. The only remaining specimen in London of Gothic and Mediæval domestic architecture	Cb	6
Crown Theatre, Peckham	Dc	13
Crystal Palace, Sydenham. Open 10 a.m. to 10 p.m. Admission 1/-. Daily Concerts and Organ Recitals, Fireworks, Aquarium, etc. (see daily papers). Headquarters of the London County Cricket Club ..	Cc	16
Cumberland Market, Regent's Park, for sale of hay	Ba	8
Custom House, Lr. Thames St. Admission to Long Room daily, 10-4 ..	Cc	6
Cutler's Hall, Warwick Lane	Ab	6
Dalston Theatre, Dalston Junction	Cb	9
Daly's Theatre, Leicester Square	Cb	7
Dartford, 11½ m. by S.E. and Chatham Ry. from Charing Cross or Ludgate Hill	Cb	5
Denmark Hill, 4 m. by S.E. and Chatham Ry. from Victoria or Ludgate Hill; also London Bridge	Cb	16
Dental Hospital, Leicester Square	Cb	7
Deptford Hospital, New Cross Road	Be	14
Deptford Park, Deptford Lower Road	Bd	14
Deptford Subway, between Deptford and Millwall, opened 1902 ..	Cd	14
Derby, The. See Epsom.		
Devonshire House, Piccadilly. London residence of the Duke of Devonshire	Bb	7
District Messenger Service. The charge is 6d. per mile; 8d. per hour. Head office, 100 St Martin's Lane	Cb	7
Downing Street, Whitehall, contains the official residences of the First Lord of the Treasury and the Chancellor of the Exchequer	Cc	7
Dog's Home, Battersea, daily, 10-4 or 6. Small gratuity	Db	12
Dorchester House, Park Lane. Fine collection of pictures shewn during the season to visitors provided with an introduction	Ab	7
Dore Gallery, 35 New Bond Street. Daily, 10 to 6, 1/-	Bb	7
Drapers' Hall, Throgmorton Street, valuable collection of paintings ..	Bb	6
Drury Lane Theatre. The oldest theatre in London, Catherine Street	Db	7

Plate No.

Dudley House, Park Lane. Fine collection of pictures shown during the season to visitors provided with an introduction .. .. .. Ab 7

Dudley Picture Gallery, Egyptian Hall, Piccadilly. Admission 1/- .. Bb 7

Duke of York's Column, Carlton House Gardens. Admission 6d. .. Bc 7

Duke of York's Military School, Chelsea, founded by the Duke of York in 1801 ; an institution where the sons of soldiers are maintained and educated ; new buildings constructing at Dover .. .. .. Da 12

Duke of York's Theatre, St Martin's Lane .. .. Cb 7

Dulwich College and Picture Gallery, contains a fine collection of pictures. Admission free from 10 to 4, 5, or 6. Closed on Sundays .. Cb 16

Dulwich Park. Opened by London County Council, 1890, 72 acres .. Cb 16

Dyers' Hall, Dowgate Hill, Cannon Street .. .. Bc 6

Earl's Court. Annual Exhibition. Great Wheel, etc. .. .. .. Ba 12

East India Docks, Blackwall, area 31¼ acres .. .. Dc 14

Eastern Empire, Bow Road .. .. Cb 14

Eden Music Hall, Little Queen Street .. .. Dc 8

Egyptian Hall, Piccadilly (now pulled down) .. .. .. Bb 7

Elephant and Castle, a well-known 'bus and car centre in South London Bb 13

Elephant and Castle Theatre, New Kent Road .. .. .. Bb 13

Eltham Palace, ¼ m. N. of Eltham sta. A favourite Royal residence from 13th to 16th cent. The remains include an old bridge, a moat still containing water, and a remarkably fine *Banqueting Hall* .. .. Cb 5

Ely Chapel, Ely Place, Holborn. The place is the site of the palace of the bishops of Ely, where John of Gaunt died in 1399. The chapel of the palace (S. Etheldreda's), now in possession of the Roman Catholics, is the only Mediæval Ecclesiastical building north of the Thames (except S. Bartholomew's, Smithfield) which escaped the great fire. The window tracery, glass, and crypt are all fine .. .. Ec 8

Empire Theatre of Varieties, Leicester Square .. .. .. Cb 7

Epping Forest, purchased by the Corporation of London, and opened by Queen Victoria in 1882, as a public park and place of recreation. The most attractive spot is High Beech, to which vehicles run from Chingford station, 6d. Good Inn at High Beech Hill .. .. Ba 5

Epsom. The great Epsom Summer Meetings, the Derby and Oaks, take place here about the end of May or beginning of June, the Derby always on a Wednesday, the Oaks on a Friday. The course may be reached by the L.B. & S.C. R. (Epsom Downs)—the S.E. & C. R. (Tattenham Corner)—the L. & S.W. (Epsom Town). Or the pedestrian, who wishes to save the heavy railway fare, may walk to the course from Betchworth sta., 4½ m. south, the walk being a charming one and mainly along turf Cc 18

Eton, 22 m. by Gt. W. Ry. Noted for its public school .. .. Ab 18

Euston Variety Theatre, Euston Road .. .. Ca 8

Evelina Hospital, for children, Southwark Bridge Road .. .. Bd 6

Exeter Hall, Strand. May meetings held here of various religious societies, generally of a Protestant character .. .. .. Db 7

Farringdon Market, Farringdon Road, for the sale of vegetables .. Ab 6

Fever Hospital, Liverpool Road, Islington, N. .. .. .. Ac 9

Farthing Down, 15 m. by S.E. and Chatham Ry. to Coulsdon station .. Bc 5

Finsbury Park, Hornsey, 115 acres, opened in 1869, cost £95,000 .. Da 10

Fire Brigade. Headquarters, Southwark Bridge Road .. .. Ca 13

Fishmongers' Hall, London Bridge. Daily .. .. Bc 6

Flaxman Gallery, University College, Gower Street. q.v. .. .. Bb 8

Foreign and India Offices, Downing Street. Fridays, 12-3, on application Cc 7

Foreign Cattle Market, Deptford .. .. Cd 14

Foresters' Music Hall, Cambridge Road, E. .. .. Ea 6

Forty Hill, Enfield, 10 m. by Gt. Northern Ry. from King's Cross .. Ba 5

Foundling Hospital, Guilford Street. Mondays, 10-4; Sundays, 11-3. Visitors, on leaving after the Sunday service, are expected to place a donation upon the plate .. .. Db 8

Fountain Fever Hospital, Tooting Grove, Lower Tooting .. .. Ab 16

Freemasons' Hall, 59 Great Queen Street. Public Meetings, Dinners, etc. Dc 8

Plate No.

French Gallery, 120 Pall Mall. Frequent exhibitions of choice pictures. Admission 1/- .. .. **Bb 7**
French Hospice, Victoria Park Road .. .. **Dc 9**
French Hospital, 172 Shaftesbury Avenue .. .. **Ca 7**
Fulham Cemetery, Fulham Palace Road .. .. **Ab 12**
Fulham Grand Theatre, Putney Bridge Station .. .. .. **Bc 12**
Fulham Palace. Residence of the Bishop of London .. .. **Ab 12**
Fulham Union, Fulham Palace Road .. .. **Aa 12**
Gadshill, near Rochester, Kent. Charles Dickens died here in 1870 .. **Cb 5**
Gaiety Theatre, 345 Strand .. .. **Db 7**
Garrick Theatre, Charing Cross Road .. .. **Cb 7**
Gatti's Music Hall, Westminster Bridge Road .. .. .. **Dc 7**
Gatti's Music Hall, Villiers Street, Strand .. .. .. **Cb 7**
General Post Office, St Martin's-le-Grand .. .. .. **Bb 6**
Geological Museum, Jermyn Street. Monday and Saturday, 10-10; other days, 10 to 4 or 5. Closed 10th August to 10th September. Free .. **Bb 7**
German Gymnastic Society, 26 Pancras Road. Introduction by a member .. .. **Ca 8**
German Hospital, Dalston Lane .. .. **Cb 9**
Gipsy Hill, 7½ m. by L.B. and S.C. Ry. from Victoria or London Bridge .. **Cc 16**
Gloucester House, Park Lane, residence of the Duke of Cambridge .. **Dc 11**
Goldsmiths' Hall, Foster Lane, behind General Post Office. Daily, 10-4; Saturdays, 10-2. Written application to Secretary of Company .. **Bb 6**
Gordon Hospital, for Fistula, Vauxhall Bridge Road .. .. .. **Ab 13**
Gordon Monument, Trafalgar Square .. .. **Cb 7**
Gordon Square Catholic Apostolic Church .. .. .. **Cb 8**
Grafton Galleries, 8 Grafton Street. January to April .. .. **Bb 7**
Grand Music Hall, Clapham .. .. **Dc 12**
Grand Theatre, High Street, Islington .. .. **Ac 9**
Granville Variety Theatre, Walham Green .. .. .. **Bb 12**
Gravesend, 30 m. by steamboat, daily from London Bridge; also by rail .. **Cb 5**
Gray's Inn, Holborn, one of the Inns of Court .. .. .. **Dc 8**
Gt. Northern Hospital, Holloway Road, N. .. ..
Gt. Scotland Yard, late the headquarters of the Metropolitan Police **Cc 7**
Gt. Queen Street Theatre .. .. **Dc 8**
Green Park, between Buckingham Palace and Piccadilly, 60 acres .. **Ac 7**
Greenwich Hospital, now the Royal Naval College. Painted Hall (Relics of Nelson) and Chapel, daily, 10-7 and 10-3; Saturdays, after 1 p.m. Hall also on Sundays, 1 p.m. Naval Museum, Ships' Models, etc., daily, Fridays and Saturdays excepted, 10-4 .. .. .. **De 14**
Greenwich Observatory, Greenwich Park. Visitors are sometimes admitted by permission of the Astronomer Royal .. .. **De 14**
Greenwich Park, 174 acres in extent, has herds of tame deer .. **De 14**
Gresham College, Basinghall Street, founded 1579 .. .. **Bb 6**
Greycoat Hospital, Westminster, a school for girls .. .. **Bd 7**
Grocers' Hall, Old Jewry .. .. **Bb 6**
Grosvenor House, Upper Grosvenor Street, residence of the Duke of Westminster .. .. **Ab 7**
Grosvenor Railway Bridge, over the Thames to Victoria Station .. **Da 12**
Guards Memorial, Waterloo Place, erected in memory of the officers and men of the Guards who fell in the Crimean War .. .. .. **Bb 7**
Guildhall. Daily, 8-5; Museum, 10-4 or 5; Free Library, 9-9 .. **Bb 6**
Guildhall School of Music, Tudor Street .. .. **Ac 6**
Guy's Hospital. Anatomical Museum, daily, 10-4, on application (professional men alone admitted) .. .. **Bd 6**
Haberdashers' Hall, Gresham Street.. .. .. **Bb 6**
Hackney Common, adjoining Victoria Park .. .. .. **Dc 9**
Hackney Congregational College, Finchley Road, erected in 1887 .. **Ab 10**
Hackney Empire, Mare Street .. .. **Cb 9**
Hackney Marsh, 337 acres in extent. Opened in 1894 as a public park .. **Eb 9**
Halkin Street Presbyterian Cha., Halkin St., Belgravia .. .. **Ac 7**

Women's archery: the competitors in action – 17th July 1908.

Plate No.

Hammersmith Bridge, between Hammersmith and Barnes. Opened in 1887 .. .. Ca 17

Hammersmith Cemetery .. .. Aa 12

Hampstead Heath, 240 acres in extent. One of the finest open spaces in London, as well as the most picturesque. A favourite holiday resort. By rail from Broad Street or Mansion House; also by tramcar. The *Vale of Health* is about half a mile from the station .. .. .. Aa 10

Hampton Court, built by Cardinal Wolsey, and presented by him to Henry VIII. in 1526. Open daily, except Friday, free, 10 a.m. to 6 p.m. April to October, and till 4 during winter, and the gardens till dusk .. Ac 17

Hanover Gallery, 47 New Bond Street, W. .. .. Aa 7

Hanwell, 12 m. by District Ry. from Mansion House; also N. London or Gt. Western Ry. .. .. Cb 18

Harrow-on-the-Hill, 15 m. by rail from Mansion House, or L. & N.W. Ry. from Euston. Noted for its public school .. .. .. Ca 18

Hatfield. A charming little town in Hertfordshire, 17½ miles from King's Cross (G.N.) Here is the fine Elizabethan mansion of the Marquis of Salisbury, standing in a noble park .. .. Ba 5

Hatton Garden, a street leading from Holborn Circus; once a fashionable residential quarter, now associated with diamond merchants .. .. Ec 8

Hayes, Middlesex, 11 m. by Gt. W. Ry. from Paddington, or District Ry. ... Ba 18

Hayes, Kent, 14 m. by S.E. and Chatham Ry. from Charing Cross or Cannon Street. Hayes Place was the seat of the Earl of Chatham, and birthplace of his son, William Pitt .. .. Bb 5

Haymarket Theatre, Haymarket .. .. Cb 7

Hendon, 8 m. by Midland Ry. from Moorgate Street and St Pancras .. Ca 18

Hengler's Circus, Argyll Street, Regent Street .. .. Ba 7

Henley, 35 m. by Gt. Western Ry. from Paddington. Regattas at end of June or beginning of July .. ..

Herald's College, Queen Victoria Street, where armorial bearings are issued Ac 6

Hertford House, Manchester Sq. Contains the Wallace Collection, q.v. Ac 8

Hick's Theatre, Shaftesbury Avenue .. .. Bb 7

High Barnet, 14 m. by Gt. Northern Ry. from King's Cross .. .. Ba 5

Highbury Fields, 27 acres in extent .. .. Ab 9

Highgate Cemetery. The most beautiful in London. Tombs of several eminent persons: Faraday, George Eliot, S. Taylor, Coleridge, etc. .. Da 18

Hippodrome, Leicester Square. Two entertainments daily, 2 and 8 p.m. Cb 7

His Majesty's Theatre, Haymarket .. .. Cb 7

Holborn Viaduct, 1400 feet long, was opened in 1869 by Queen Victoria Ec 8

Holloway College for Women, near Egham; a school of the University of London, founded in 1883 by the late Mr Thomas Holloway. Admission to College and Picture Gallery, by order from the Secretary .. .. Ab 18

Holloway Empire Theatre, Holloway Road .. .. Da 10

Holloway Prison, Camden Road .. .. Cb 10

Homœopathic Hospital, Great Ormond Street, W.C. .. .. Cb 8

Honourable Artillery Company. The armoury and parade-grounds are near Bunhill Fields, Finsbury .. .. Ba 6

Horniman's Museum, Forest Hill, gifted by Mr Horniman in 1901. Open, free, daily, 2 to 9, including Sundays .. .. Cb 16

Hornsey, 5½ m. by Gt. N. Ry. from Moorgate Street or Midland Railway Da 18

Horse Guards, Whitehall. Headquarters of the Commander in Chief of the British Army .. .. Cc 7

Horticultural Society's Gardens, Chiswick. The experimental gardens were removed in 1904 to Wisley, Surrey .. ..

Hounslow Heath, has extensive barracks for both cavalry and infantry Bb 18

Houses of Parliament, Westminster.—By ticket obtainable at the Lord Chamberlain's Office in the Victoria Tower. The Houses may be viewed on Saturdays, free from 10-4. A member's order is required to admit strangers during the debates .. .. Cc 7

Hoxton Music Hall, Hoxton Street, N. .. .. Bc 9

	Plate No.
Hyde Park, 480 acres in extent. The most fashionable park in London ..	Dc **11**
Imperial Institute, South Kensington.—Open free from 10 to 4 or 5 ..	Cd **11**
Imperial Theatre, Tothill Street, Westminster	Cc **7**
India Museum, South Kensington. Daily, 10-4. Free all the week ..	Cc **11**
Inland Revenue Office, Somerset House, Strand	Db **7**
Inns of Court. Comprise the Inner Temple, Middle Temple, Lincoln's Inn, and Gray's Inn	Dc **8**
Institute of Journalists, Tudor Street	Eb **7**
Institution of Civil Engineers, 25 Gt. George Street, Westminster ..	Cc **7**
Ironmongers' Hall, Fenchurch Street	Cc **6**
Isleworth, 12 m. by S. W. Ry. from Waterloo, Ludgate Hill, or Broad St.	Aa **17**
Isle of Dogs, between Limehouse and Blackwall	Cd **14**
Italian Hospital, 40 and 41 Queen's Square, W.C.	Cb **8**
Jack Straw's Castle, Hampstead Heath. An interesting old inn. Point where the Essex peasants encamped on their march to join Wat Tyler approaching from Kent	Aa **10**
Kempton Park, near Sunbury. Races and Steeplechases	Bb **18**
Kennington Oval. Headquarters of the Surrey County Cricket Club ..	Bc **13**
Kennington Park, Kennington Park Road	Bc **13**
Kennington Theatre, Kennington Park Road	Bb **13**
Kensal Green Cemetery. Tombs of several eminent persons, Brunel, Tom Hood, Sydney Smith, Thackeray, etc.	Aa **11**
Kensington Congregational Chapel, Allen Street	Bc **11**
Kensington Gardens, over 200 acres in extent	Cc **11**
Kensington Palace. Birth-place of Queen Victoria	Cc **11**
Kew Gardens, by rail from Broad St., Moorgate St., Waterloo, Ludgate Hill, or Mansion House ; or by steamer to Kew Pier. Open, free, daily from 10 till dusk ; Sunday afternoons, 1 p.m. Closed on Christmas day ..	Ba **17**
King's College, forms part of Somerset House, built by Smirke in 1828. Is a school of the London University. The museum contains a collection of models and instruments. Admission by introduction from a member..	Db **7**
King's College Hospital, Carey Street, Lincoln's Inn	Dc **8**
Kingston-upon-Thames, 12 m. by S.-W. Ry., from Waterloo ; or by water. Several Saxon kings were crowned here, the first being Athelstane, in 924	Bc **17**
Knightsbridge Barracks (Cavalry), Hyde Park	Dc **11**
Knockholt Beeches, 3 m. from Halstead Sta., S. E., and C. Ry. ..	Cc **5**
Lady Couriers, 4 Charing Cross	Cb **7**
Lambeth Bridge, between Pimlico and Lambeth, opened in 1862 ..	Ab **13**
Lambeth Palace, for over 600 years the official residence of the Archbishop of Canterbury. A portion of the Palace Grounds was opened to the public in 1900	Bb **13**
Lansdowne House, Berkeley Square, contains a valuable collection of pictures, and Roman Sculptures	Ab **7**
Law Courts, see Royal Courts of Justice	Da **7**
Leadenhall Market, Leadenhall Street. For Meat, Poultry, and Game	Cc **6**
Leathersellers' Hall, St Helen's Place, Bishopsgate Street	Cb **6**
Leith Hill, (965 ft.) Surrey, 5 m. from Dorking, L.B. & S.C. Ry. Fourteen Counties visible from the Tower	Bc **5**
Leighton House, Holland Park. Collection of pictures by Lord Leighton	Bc **11**
Lemercier Gallery, 35 New Bond Street. Daily, 1s.	Bb **7**
Leyton, 6 m. by rail from Liverpool St., or Fenchurch St., or from St Pancras. The Essex County Cricket Ground is within a mile of the station	Bb **5**
Lillie Bridge, West Brompton, cricket and athletic sports	Ba **12**
Limpsfield, Surrey, 20 m. by L. B. & S. C. Ry. to Oxted Station. Golf links and cricket ground	Bc **5**
Lincoln's Inn Fields, taken over by the London County Council, and opened as a public recreation ground in 1895	Dc **8**
Lincoln's Inn, one of the Inns of Court	Dc **8**
Linnæan Society, Burlington House, Piccadilly	Bb **7**

Plate No.

Lloyd's, Royal Exchange, Cornhill. Where the business of underwriting, or naval insurance, is conducted .. .. Bc 6

Lloyd's Register, 71 Fenchurch Street, for the classification of ships .. Cc 6

London Bridge. The most important of the bridges over the Thames in London. Connects the City with the Borough on the south side; completed in 1831. 928 ft. long and 65 ft. broad .. .. .. Bc 6

London County Council Offices, Spring Gardens. Council created by the Local Government Act of 1888. Comprises 118 Councillors and 19 Aldermen appointed by the Council .. .. Cb 7

London Docks, Wapping; Western Dock, 20 acres; Eastern Dock, 6 acres Dc 6

London Fever Hospital, Liverpool Road .. .. Ac 9

London Fields, Hackney; a public park .. .. Cc 9

London Hospital, Whitechapel Road .. .. Eb 6

London Missionary Society's Museum, 14 Blomfield Street, Finsbury. Daily, 10-4; Saturdays, 10-2 .. .. Cb 6

London Music Hall, 95 High Street, Shoreditch .. .. .. Bd 9

London Stone, St Swithin's Church, Cannon Street .. .. .. Bc 6

London Pavilion (Music Hall), Piccadilly Circus .. .. .. Bb 7

London Wall. Remains of the ancient wall that surrounded London can be seen in the churchyard of St Alphage, Aldermanbury .. .. Bb 6

Long Gallery, 168 New Bond Street. Admission 1/- .. .. .. Bb 7

Lord's Cricket Ground, St John's Wood. Headquarters of the Marylebone and Middlesex Cricket Club .. .. Ac 10

Lost Property Office, New Scotland Yard, Victoria Embankment .. Cc 7

Lyceum Theatre, Wellington Street, Strand .. .. Db 7

Lyric Opera House, Hammersmith .. .. Aa 12

Lyric Theatre, Shaftesbury Avenue .. .. Bb 7

Maidenhead, Berks, 26 m. by Gt. Western Ry., from Paddington .. Aa 18

Mansion House. The official residence of the Lord Mayor, with so-called Egyptian Hall. On application .. .. Bc 6

Marble Arch. At the N.E. or Cumberland Gate entrance to Hyde Park; after the style of the Arch of Constantine, was originally erected by George IV. as the principal entrance to Buckingham Palace .. .. Dc 11

Marlborough House, on East side of St James' Palace, is the town residence of the Prince of Wales. Built by Wren in 1709 .. .. Bc 7

Marlborough Street Police Court, Gt. Marlborough St. .. .. Bc 8

Marlborough Theatre, Holloway .. .. Db 10

Marylebone Theatre, Church Street .. .. Cb 11

Marylebone Workhouse, Marylebone Road .. .. .. Ab 8

Maryon Park, Charlton, near Woolwich .. .. Cb 15

Mercers' Hall, Ironmonger Lane, Cheapside .. .. Bb 6

Merchant Tailors' Hall, Threadneedle Street .. .. .. Cb 6

Meteorological Office, Victoria Street, Westminster. Forecasts of the weather may be obtained, daily, 11 to 8; Sundays, 7 to 8 p.m. Fee, 1/- Bd 7

Metropole Theatre, Camberwell Green .. .. Cc 13

Metropolitan Cattle Market, Islington. Principal days, Mondays and Thursdays .. .. Cb 10

Metropolitan Hospital, Kingsland Road, N.E. .. .. .. Bc 9

Metropolitan Meat Market.—Poultry, Fish; Smithfield .. .. Ab 6

Metropolitan Music Hall, Edgware Road .. .. Cb 11

Middlesex Hospital, Mortimer Street .. .. Bc 8

Middlesex Music Hall, Drury Lane .. .. Cc 8

Merchant Tailors' Schools, Charterhouse .. .. Aa 6

Metropolitan Tabernacle (Spurgeon's), Newington Butts .. .. Bb 13

Millwall Docks, Isle of Dogs .. .. Cd 14

Mitcham Common, about 8 m. by S. W. Ry., from Waterloo .. .. Bc 16

Montague House, Whitehall, residence of the Duke of Buccleuch .. Cc 7

Monument, The, Fish Street Hill.—Erected in commemoration of the Great Fire of 1666. Daily, Sundays excepted. Admission, 3d. .. Cc 6

Moore & Burgess's (Christy) **Minstrels.** St James' Hall, Piccadilly Bb 7

Moravian Chapel, Fetter Lane. Of historic interest .. .. .. Ec 8

Olympic Tug of War Competition.

Plate No.

Mortlake, 8½ m. by rail from Waterloo, or Ludgate Hill. The Oxford and Cambridge annual boat race from Putney, finishes here   .. ..   **Ba 17**

Museum of Building Appliances, 9 Conduit Street ; Regent Street. Daily, on application   .. ..   **Bb 7**

National Gallery, Trafalgar Square. Monday, Tuesday, Wednesday, and Saturday, 10 to 4, 5, or 6. Free. Closed during October   .. **Cb 7**

National Gallery of British Art (Tate Gallery), Grosvenor Road. Same hours as National Gallery   .. ..   **Ab 13**

National Portrait Gallery, St Martin's Place, Charing Cross   .. **Cb 7**

Natural History Museum, South Kensington. Daily, 10 to 4, 5, or 6. Free   .. ..   **Cd 11**

Nelson's Column, Trafalgar Square, 145 feet in height. Erected in 1843, at a cost of £45,000   .. ..   **Cb 7**

New Cross Music Hall, New Cross Road   .. ..   **Ce 14**

New Gallery, Regent Street. Modern Pictures. Open 10-6. Admission 1/-   **Bb 7**

New Theatre, St Martin's Lane   .. ..   **Cb 7**

New Scotland Yard, Victoria Embankment, headquarters of the Metropolitan Police   .. ..   **Cc 7**

New Pavilion Music Hall, Mile End Road   .. ..   **Db 6**

New Sadler's Wells Music Hall, Arlington Street   .. .. ..   **Ea 8**

North Eastern Hospital for Children, Hackney Road, E.   .. .. **Cc 9**

North Western Fever Hospital, Lawn Road, Hampstead   .. .. **Bb 10**

Northampton Institute, St John's St. Road. Largest polytechnic in London   .. ..   **Eb 8**

Norwood, 7 m. by L.B. & S.C. Ry. In Norwood Cemetery Douglas Jerrold is buried   .. ..   **Cc 16**

Obelisk, St George's Circus, Borough. Erected in 1771 to commemorate Lord Mayor Crosby, who was instrumental in obtaining the release of a printer who was imprisoned for publishing the parliamentary debates   .. **Bb 13**

Olympia, Addison Road, Kensington. Exhibitions, Shows, Sports, etc.   ..   **Bd 11**

Omnibuses. The routes clearly indicated by colour on the maps, and a detailed list will be found on pages 26-29.

Orpington and the Crays, 15 m. by S.E. and Chatham Ry. from Charing Cross or Cannon Street   .. ..   **Cb 5**

Orthopædic Hospital, 297 Oxford Street, W. ..   ..   **Bc 8**

Ottershaw Park, Surrey, by S. Western Ry. from Waterloo to Addleston Station. The park is 2 m. from the station   .. ..   **Ab 5**

Oxford Music Hall, Oxford Street   .. ..   **Cc 8**

Oxshott Heath, 14 m. by S. Western Ry. from Waterloo   .. .. **Cc 18**

Paddington Green Hospital (St Mary's) ..   ..   **Cb 11**

Paddington Recreation Ground, Kilburn Park   .. .. ..   **Ba 11**

Palace Music Hall, Shaftesbury Avenue   .. ..   **Cb 7**

Panshanger Park, Herts., 28 m. by Gt. N. Ry., near Cole Green station   **Ba 5**

Paragon Theatre of Varieties, Mile End Road   .. .. ..   **Bb 14**

Parcel Post Office, Mount Pleasant, Farringdon Road, on the site of the old Coldbath House of Correction   .. ..   **Db 8**

Park Square Baptist Chapel, Regent's Park   .. .. ..   **Db 11**

Parkes' Museum of Hygiene, Margaret Street. Open on week-days, 10-6   **Bc 8**

Parliament Hill, Hampstead, 265 acres in extent ; highest point, 319 ft. ..   **Ba 10**

Passmore Edwards Hall, Clare Market. London School of Economics   **Da 7**

Passmore Edwards Sailors' Palace, West India Dock Road, E. ..   **Bc 14**

Patent Museum, South Kensington. Daily, 10 to 5, free   .. ..   **Cc 11**

Patent Office, Chancery Lane ; for the protection of patents and designs, also for the protection of trade marks   .. ..   **Dc 8**

Peabody Buildings. These are buildings erected by the Peabody trust for the working classes residing in the metropolis. The average weekly rent for each family is about 4s. 9d., which includes the use of baths and wash-houses. The number of persons accommodated is about 20,000. The capital fund is now about £1,250,000, Peabody's own contributions having exceeded £500,000. His statue is in Threadneedle Street, behind the Exchange   .. ..   **Bc 6**

Plate No.

Peckham Rye and Park, two of the best known open spaces in the southern suburbs .. .. **Cb 16**

Pentonville Prison, Caledonian Road .. .. .. **Db 10**

People's Palace, Mile End Road. Opened by Queen Victoria in 1887 .. **Bb 14**

Petersham Park, Surrey, near Richmond .. .. **Ab 17**

Petticoat Lane, Whitechapel. Re-named Middlesex Street. An extensive business is done here on Sunday mornings, and is one of the sights of the East End .. .. **Cb 6**

Playhouse, Northumberland Avenue .. .. **Cb 7**

Plumstead Common, near Woolwich .. .. **Ec 15**

Poet's Corner, S. Transept of Westminster Abbey, where many celebrated poets are buried .. .. **Cc 7**

Polytechnic Young Men's Christian Institute, Regent Street .. **Bc 8**

Poplar Hospital, East India Dock Road .. .. **Cc 14**

Portman Chapel, Portman Square .. .. **Db 11**

Portman Market, Church Street, Marylebone .. .. .. **Cb 11**

Portman Rooms, Baker Street .. .. **Ac 8**

Preceptors, College of. An examining institute which grants diplomas to teachers, Bloomsbury Square .. .. **Cc 8**

Primrose Hill, 219 ft. high, lies to the north of Regent's Park .. **Bc 10**

Prince of Wales's Theatre, Coventry Street.. .. .. . **Cb 7**

Prince's Hall, 191 Piccadilly. Concerts, Meetings, etc. .. .. **Bb 7**

Princess's Theatre, 152 Oxford Street .. .. **Bc 8**

Public Record's Office, Fetter Lane .. .. **Dc 8**

Purfleet, Essex, 15 m. by Tilbury and Southend Ry. from Fenchurch St. stn. **Cb 5**

Putney, Surrey, 5 m. by rail from Waterloo ; also by steamboat. Starting-point of Oxford and Cambridge annual boat race .. .. .. **Cb 17**

Queen Charlotte Hospital, with Nurses' Home, Marylebone Road .. **Db 11**

Queen's Hall, Langham Place. Promenade Concerts .. .. .. **Bc 8**

Queen's Music Hall, Poplar .. .. **Cb 14**

Queen's Theatre, Lavender Hill, S.W. .. .. **Cc 12**

Railway Clearing House, Seymour Street .. .. **Ba 8**

Raphael Gallery, 4 Cockspur Street, Charing Cross. Open 10 to 6, 1/- .. **Cb 7**

Regalia or Crown Jewels are kept in the Tower of London. q.v. .. **Cc 6**

Regent's Park, 472 acres in extent, contains, the Zoological Gardens with the finest collection of wild beasts and birds in the world. Also the Botanical Gardens, with a large conservatory, and a large portion of ground laid out with a choice collection of trees, shrubs, and flowers .. **Aa 8**

Reigate, Surrey, 24 m. by S. E. and Chatham Ry., from London Bridge **Bc 5**

Religious Tract Society, 56 Paternoster Row .. .. .. **Ab 6**

Richmond, 10 m. by rail from Waterloo, Broad St., or Mansion House Stations, by water Steamboat. *Richmond Hill*, with fine view, and *Park* of 2253 acres ; also the Pen Ponds .. .. **Bb 17**

Rickmansworth, 18 miles from Baker St., a centre for many beautiful excursions. 4½ m. W. is *Chalfont St. Giles.* In this pretty village is the cottage where Milton finished "Paradise Lost" and began "Paradise Regained." (Admission 6d.) About 2 miles to the south is the interesting old Quaker meeting-house of *Jordans*, a pilgrimage place for Americans. Here are the graves of Elwood (Milton's secretary); William Penn (d. 1718), his wife, and five children. Two miles beyond is the lovely little town of Beaconsfield. An extension may be made via *Stoke Pogis*, the scene of Gray's *Elegy*, with the tomb of the poet, winding up at Slough (2 miles). The entire walk or ride from Rickmansworth to Slough (18 miles) probably combines more beauty and literary interest than any other in England .. .. .. **Aa 5**

Riddlesdown, Surrey, 15 m. by S. E. and Chatham Ry., or L. B. and S. C. Ry., to Upper Warlingham Station. Favourite picnic resort .. **Bc 5**

Rosherville Gardens, near Gravesend, by steamer .. .. .. **Cb 5**

Rotten Row.—Probably a corruption of "route du roi." . A track in Hyde Park from Hyde Park Corner to Kensington Gate (1½ m.) exclusively reserved for riders .. .. **Cc 11**

Plate No.

Rowton Houses.—These were established by Lord Rowton in 1893, to provide a series of "Poor Man's Hotels." At present there are 5 houses, situated at Vauxhall, King's Cross, Newington Butts, Hammersmith, and Whitechapel.

Royal Academy, Burlington House, Piccadilly. Exhibition of Paintings, May to July. Admission 1/- ; evenings, 6d. ..   ..   ..   Bb   7

Royal Academy of Music, South Tenterden Street, Hanover Square   ..   Ac   8

Royal Albert Dock, North Woolwich. Area, 72 acres ..   ..   Ca   15

Royal Asiatic Society, 22 Albemarle Street   ..   ..   ..   Bb   7

Royal Astronomical Society, Burlington House   ..   ..   Bb   7

Royal Arcade, between Old Bond Street and Albemarle Street ..   Bb   7

Royal College of Music, Prince Consort Road   Cc   11

Royal College of Physicians, Trafalgar Square   ..   ..   Cb   7

Royal Courts of Justice, Strand. Open Free during the sittings   ..   Da   7

Royal Ear Hospital, 66 Frith Street, Soho   ..   ..   Ca   7

Royal Exchange, Cornhill, opened by Queen Victoria in 1844. Free daily, 3.30-4.30 p.m.   Cc   6

Royal Eye Hospital, St George's Circus, Blackfriar's Road   ..   Bb   13

Royal Free Hospital, 256 Gray's Inn Road   ..   ..   ..   Db   8

Royal Geographical Society, 1 Savile Row ..   ..   ..   Bb   7

Royal Historical Society, 115 St Martin's Lane   ..   ..   Cb   7

Royal Hospital for children and women, 51 Waterloo Bridge Road   ..   Dc   7

Royal Humane Society, 4 Trafalgar Square. Founded in 1774.   ..   Cb   7

Royal Institution, 21 Albemarle Street, Piccadilly   ..   ..   Bb   7

Royal Institute of Painters in Water Colours, 191 Piccadilly, W., April to July, 1/- ..   ..   Bb   7

Royal Mews.—Shown by application to the Master of the Horse   ..   Ad   7

Royal Mint, Tower Hill. Admission on written application to Deputy Master   ..   ..   Dc   6

Royal Music Hall, 242 High Holborn ..   ..   Dc   8

Royal National Life Boat Institution, 14 John Street, Adelphi   ..   Cb   7

Royal Naval College, See Greenwich Hospital   ..   ..   Ce   14

Royal Normal College for the Blind, Upper Norwood   Cc   16

Royal Society.—Occupies part of the east wing of Burlington House. The society—the most important of the learned bodies of Gt. Britain—was founded in 1660, and received its charter of incorporation in 1663. It comprises over 500 members   ..   ..   ..   Bb   7

Royal Society of Painters in Water Colours, 5a Pall Mall, E. Admission, 1/- ..   ..   Bc   7

Royal Statistical Society, Adelphi Terrace   ..   ..   ..   Db   7

Royal Victualling Yard, Deptford ..   ..   Bd   14

Royalty Theatre, 73 Dean Street, Soho   ..   ..   ..   Ba   7

Rye House, Herts, 18 m. by Gt. Eastern Ry. from Liverpool St. Station. The meeting place of the Rye House conspirators (1683). Built in the reign of Henry VI., it afterwards passed into private hands, and is now a hotel, and a favourite summer resort   ..   ..   ..   Ba   5

Saddlers' Hall, Cheapside   ..   ..   Bb   6

St Alban's Church, Brook Street, Holborn. One of the leading churches of the advanced type   ..   ..   Dc   8

St Alban's Church, Baldwin's Gardens   ..   ..   ..   Dc   8

St Andrew's Church, Holborn Viaduct. Built by Wren   ..   Ec   8

St Andrew's Church, Wells Street, Oxford Street. Noted for its music   Bc   8

St Anne's Church, Wardour Street, Soho. Noted for its music   ..   Bb   7

St Augustine's Church, Kilburn Park Road. Perhaps the most imposing of modern London churches..

St Bartholomew's Church, Smithfield. With the exception of the chapel in the Tower, which is 20 years earlier, this is the oldest church in London. It was founded by Rahere in 1123, and is a fine specimen of pure Norman work, of peculiar interest to antiquarians and ecclesiologists   Ab   6

St Bartholomew's Hospital, Smithfield. Anatomical museum, daily, 10-4, Thursdays excepted. Also paintings by Hogarth. On application   Ab   6

Henry Taylor, Triple Gold Medal Winner for Swimming (400m, 1500m and 4x200 m. Freestyle Swimming Event).

Plate No.

St Benet's Church, Mile End Road .. .. Dd 9

St Bride's Church, Fleet Street. In the centre aisle is the grave of Richardson (d. 1761), the author of "Clarissa Harlow" .. .. Ec 8

St Clement Danes, Strand. On the supposed burial place of Harold Harefoot and other Danes. A tablet on his pew records that Dr Johnson worshipped here .. .. Db 7

St Columba's Church (Church of Scotland), Pont Street, Belgravia .. Dd 11

St Dunstan's Church, Fleet Street. The statue of Queen Elizabeth over the Vestry door once stood on the old Lud-Gate, at the foot of Ludgate Hill Ea 7

St Ethelburga's Church, Bishopsgate Street. One of the oldest and one of the smallest churches in London, ... Cb 6

St George's R.C. Cathedral, Southwark. By Pugin (1840-1848) .. Ed 7

St George's Church, Hanover Square. Noted for the great number of fashionable marriages which are celebrated within it .. .. .. Bb 7

St George's Hall, Langham Place .. .. Bc 8

St George's Hill and Cæsar's Camp, Surrey, 1¼ m. S.E. of Weybridge Bc 18

St George's Hospital, Hyde Park Corner, W. .. .. .. Ac 7

St Giles's, Cripplegate. 14th Century. Tombs of John Milton (d. 1674); Foxe, the Martyrologist (d. 1587); Martin Frobisher (d. 1594); and Speed the Topographer (d. 1629). Oliver Cromwell was married here (Aug. 22nd, 1620), and the register has the entry of the burial of Daniel Defoe (d. 1731). In the churchyard is an old bastion of London Wall .. Bb 6

St Helen's Church, Bishopsgate. Contains many memorials to well known Londoners, etc. .. .. Cb 6

St James's Church, Piccadilly. By Wren (1682-84). Foliage over the altar, and font, by Grinling Gibbons .. .. Bb 7

St James's Hall, Langham Street, to be built on site of St Paul's Church Bc 8

St James's Home, Fulham Palace Road. One of the most important rescue places in London .. .. Ab 12

St James's Park. Area about 90 acres, is one of the most interesting parks in London. The artificial sheet of water is a favourite skating place in winter .. .. Bc 7

St James's Palace, where Queen Victoria and Prince Albert were married Bc 7

St James's Theatre, King Street .. .. Bc 7

St John's Gate, St John's Lane, Clerkenwell. A relic of the old priory of the Knights of St John, with turrets (1504). The Norman crypt of St John's Church is part of the old priory, and associated with the exposure of the "Cock Lane Ghost." In the graveyard are buried some relatives of Wilkes Booth, the assassin of President Lincoln .. .. .. Aa 6

St John's Hospital, Leicester Square. For diseases of the skin .. Cb 7

St Katherine's Dock. Area about 12 acres .. .. Dc 6

St Lawrence Church, Jewry. By Wren (1671-80), with tomb of Abp. Tillotson (d. 1694) .. .. : .. .. Cc 6

St Luke's Hospital, Old Street, City Road .. .. Bd 9

St Margaret's Church, Westminster. Built in the reign of Edward I., on the site of an earlier church of Edward the Confessor, and improved under Edward IV. William Caxton, Sir Walter Raleigh, and Admiral Blake were buried here .. .. Cc 7

St Martin's in the Fields Church. By Gibbs (1721-26). Nell Gwynne (d. 1687), Farquhar the dramatist (d. 1707), and Roubiliac the sculptor (d. 1762), were buried in the churchyard .. .. Cb 7

St Mary's Church, Aldermanbury. Tomb of the infamous Judge Jeffreys (d. 1689). Milton's second marriage took place here in 1656 .. Bb 6

St Mary's (le Bow), Cheapside. One of Wren's best churches. The true "Cockney" is supposed to be born within the sound of its bells .. Bc 6

St Mary Magdalene's Church, Paddington. One of the most important modern churches in London, now possesses a most exquisite crypt un-equalled in London .. .. Cb 11

St Mary-le-Strand. By Gibbs (1717). S. Thomas à Becket was rector of the parish in the reign of Stephen .. .. Db 7

St Mary Woolnoth Church, Lombard Street .. .. .. Bc 6

Plate No.

St Michael's Church, Chester Square, Pimlico	Ad	7
St Michael's Church, Cornhill. The wood carvings by Grinling Gibbons	Cc	6
St Olave's Church, Hart Street, Mark Lane. Tombs of Samuel Pepys (d. 1703), and his wife, who worshipped here	Cc	6
St Pancras Church, Euston Road. An imitation of the Erechtheum at Athens	Cb	8
St Paul's Cathedral. On week-days, 7.45 a.m. till dusk. Divine Service —8, 10 a.m. 1.15, 4, and 7 p.m. ; Sundays—8, 10.30 a.m., 3.15 and 7 p.m. Area, free; Whispering Gallery, 6d. ; Golden Gallery, 1/-; Ball, 1/6; Library, Bell, and Geometrical Staircase, 6d. ; Clock, 2d. ; Crypt, 6d. ..	Ab	6
St Paul's Church, Covent Garden. Originally built by Inigo Jones in 1663	Cb	7
St Paul's Church, Wilton Place, Knightsbridge	Dc	11
St Paul's Church, Lorrimore Square, Walworth	Bb	13
St Paul's Schools. Founded in 1512, and removed to Hammersmith in 1884	Aa	12
St Saviour's Church, Southwark. More correctly, *St Mary Overies'*. The cathedral church of South London. Fragments of the original Norman nave still exist. The choir and Lady Chapel were built in 1207	Ca	13
St Saviour's Hospital, Osnaburgh Street (for cancer). The chapel contains some of the finest wood-carving to be found in England	Bb	8
St Sepulchre's Church, Holborn Viaduct. Roger Ascham, the tutor of Lady Jane Grey, is buried here (d. 1568)	Ec	8
St Stephen's Church, Gloucester Road, S. Kensington	Ca	12
St Stephen's Church, Walbrook. By Wren	Bc	6
St Thomas's Hospital, on Albert Embankment, opposite Houses of Parliament	Dc	7
Salvation Army Headquarters, 101 Queen Victoria Street	Bc	6
Sandown Park, 14 m. from Waterloo Station. Races	Cc	18
Savoy Theatre, Beaufort Buildings, Strand	Db	7
Scala Theatre, Charlotte Street, W.	Bc	8
Serpentine. An artificial lake in Hyde Park	Cc	11
Sevenoaks, 22 m. from Charing Cross, Victoria, or Ludgate Hill ..	Cc	5
Shadwell Market, for the sale of fish, Shadwell, E.	Ac	14
Shaftesbury Home, Shaftesbury Avenue. A home for destitute boys ..	Ca	7
Shaftesbury Theatre, Shaftesbury Avenue	Cb	7
Shaftesbury Training Ship, lies in the Thames off Grays	Cb	5
Shakespeare Theatre, Clapham Junction		
Sheerness, I. of Sheppey. A fortified dockyard and garrison town ..	Db	5
Shirley Hills, Surrey. 2 m. from S. Croydon Sta., L. B. & S. C. Ry. ..	Dc	18
Sick Children's Hospital, Great Ormond Street, W.C.	Db	8
Sir James Cass Technical Institute, Jewry Street	Cc	6
Sion College Library, Thames Embankment	Eb	7
Sion House, Brentford. A house of very great historic interest	Aa	17
Skinners' Hall, Dowgate, Cannon Street	Bc	6
Smithfield Hay Market, Smithfield	Ab	6
Snaresbrook, 8 m. by Gt. E. Ry., from Liverpool St., or N. London Ry.	Bb	5
Soane's Museum, 13 Lincoln's Inn Fields. Free, on application, on Tuesdays and Thursdays in February and March, and on Tuesdays, Wed., Thur., and Fri. during remainder of year, from 11 till 5 ..	Dc	8
Society for Promoting Christian Knowledge, Northumberland Av.	Cb	7
Society of British Artists, 6 Suffolk Street, Pall Mall East. Admission, 1/-	Cb	7
Soldiers' Daughters' Home, Rosslyn Hill, Hampstead	Ab	10
Somerset House, Strand. Now devoted to Inland Revenue Office, Exchequer and Audit, Registry of Wills, Births, Deaths, &c.	Db	7
Southend-on-Sea, Essex. 40 m. by Gt. E. Ry., from Liverpool St. ..	Db	5
South London Fish Market, New Kent Road	Cb	13
South London Music Hall, London Road, S.E.	Bb	13
Southwark Bridge, between Blackfriars and London Bridges	Bc	6
Southwark Park, near the Surrey Commercial Docks. Area 63 acres.	Ad	14
Spitalfields Market. Vegetables, etc. The great emporium of East London	Cb	6

Plate No.

Stafford House, St James's Park. Residence of the Duke of Sutherland Bc 7
Staines.—A picturesque old town on the Thames, with Stations on the
G. W. & L. & S.W. Ry. Not far away lies *Runimede*, where King
John signed Magna Charta (1215); while above the town is *Cooper's
Hill*, celebrated by Denman, with the Royal Indian Engineering Col-
lege, established 1870 .. .. Bb 18
Standard Music Hall, Victoria Street, Westminster .. .. .. Bd 7
Standard Theatre, High St., Shoreditch .. .. Ca 6
Stationers' Hall, Stationers' Hall Court. For copyright registry .. Ab 6
Steinway Hall, 15 Lower Seymour Street, Portman Square .. .. Ac 8
Stock Exchange, Capel Court, Bartholomew Lane, Cheapside .. .. Bb 6
Strand Theatre, 168 Strand .. .. Db 7
Strawberry Hill, between Teddington and Twickenham. The famous
villa of Horace Walpole .. .. Ab 17
Streatham Common, 8 m. by rail from Victoria or London Bridge .. Bc 16
Surbiton, near Kingston, on the L. & S.W. Ry., 12 miles from London .. Bc 17
Surgeons' Museum, Lincoln's Inn Fields. Mondays, Tuesdays, Wednes-
days, and Thursdays, 12-5. Closed during September. By order of a
member of the Royal College of Surgeons, or by application at
Museum .. .. Dc 8
Surrey Commercial Docks, Rotherhithe. Chiefly used for timber .. Bc 14
Surrey Theatre, 124, Blackfriars Road .. .. Ed 7
Tate Gallery. See National Gallery of British Art .. .. .. Ab 13
Tattersall's, Knightsbridge, the most important horse auction mart in
London .. .. Dc 11
Teddington, 18 m. by river or 14 m. by S.W. Ry. from Waterloo .. Ab 17
Telegraph Hill, Hatcham. Opened to the public in 1895 .. .. Ca 16
Temple, The, formerly a lodge of the Knights Templars, established to
protect the Holy Sepulchre. On the dissolution of the Order in 1313, it
was presented to the Earl of Pembroke, after whose death it passed to
the Knights of St John, who leased it (1346) to the students of common
law .. .. Eb 7
Temple Bar Memorial, Fleet Street. Erected in 1880 to mark the site of
Temple Bar, a gateway built by Wren in 1670. The original gate now
stands near one of the entrances of Theobald's Park .. .. .. Db 7
Temple Church.—There are two portions of this well known Church, the
Round Church, a Norman structure finished in 1185, with nine monu-
ments of Templars of the 12th and 13th centuries; and the *Choir*. The
incumbent of the Temple Church is styled the Master of the Temple Db 7
Terriss's Theatre, Deptford Lower Road .. .. Bd 14
Terry's Theatre, 105 Strand .. .. Db 7
Thames Tunnel, between Wapping and Rotherhithe; used by the East
London Railway .. .. Ed 6
Thavies' Inn, Holborn, one of the Inns of Chancery .. .. .. Dc 8
Tilbury, 3 m. by Gt. E. Ry. from Liverpool Street; also by North London
Ry., Extensive Docks .. .. Cb 5
Tilbury Fort. Built by Henry VIII., to defend the mouth of the Thames,
and afterwards added to and strengthened. Here Elizabeth reviewed
her troops in anticipation of the Armada (1588) .. .. .. Cb 5
Tivoli Theatre of Varieties, Strand .. .. Cb 7
Tooting Common, may be reached by L.B. and S. Coast Ry. .. .. Bb 16
Tower Bridge. Opened 1894; cost £750,000 .. .. Cc 6
Tower Hamlets and City of London Cemetery, Mile End .. .. Cb 14
Tower Hill, N.W. of the Tower. Here formerly stood the scaffold for
the execution of traitors .. .. Cc 6
Tower of London. Containing regalia, etc. Mondays and Saturdays,
free; other days, 1/-. Armouries, 6d.; Jewels, 6d. .. .. .. Cc 6
Tower Subway. Opened in 1870, but closed to passengers in 1897 .. Cc 6
Toynbee Hall, Commercial Street, Whitechapel. Founded in 1895. A
centre of the University Extension Lectures' schemes .. .. Db 6
Toxopholite (Archery) Society, Regent's Park .. .. .. Db 11

Dancing Queens: Danish gymnasts perform an acrobatic routine.

Plate No.

Trafalgar Square.—Begun in 1831, and named after Nelson's crowning victory. The great feature of the square is the Nelson Column, 145 feet high, copied from one of the columns of the temple of Mars Ultor at Rome .. .. Cb 7

Treasury, The, between Horse Guards and Downing Street .. .. Cc 7

Trinity Alms Houses, Mile End Road .. .. Ab 14

Trinity Church, Minories .. .. Cc 6

Trinity House, Tower Hill. Admission by ticket, obtainable from the secretary .. .. Cc 6

Tussaud's (Madame) Exhibition, Marylebone Road, adjoining Baker Street Station. Open 10 to 10. In the evening, music. Collection of wax figures, etc. Admission 1/-; Chamber of Horrors, 6d. extra .. Ab 8

Twickenham, 11½ m. by S. W. Ry. from Waterloo. The villa of the poet Pope is here .. .. Ab 17

Tyburn (Tree).—This notorious place of execution lay at the lower corner of Edgware Road, almost opposite the Marble Arch .. .. Db 11

United Service Museum, Whitehall, given by Queen Victoria in 1893 for a museum of National treasures connected with Army and Navy; daily, 6d. Cc 7

University Boat Race.—Is rowed annually just before Easter, from Putney to Mortlake, between crews of eights chosen from the two universities. The best view is at the bend of the river near Barnes Bridge .. Cb 17

University College Hospital, Gower Street .. .. .. Bb 8

University College Museum, Gower Street. Flaxman Museum, Saturdays, 10-4, from May to August. On application to gatekeeper .. Bb 8

University of London, lately at Burlington House, now at Imperial Institute .. .. Cd 11

Variety Music Hall, 20 Pitfield Street, Hoxton .. .. .. Bd 9

Vaudeville Theatre, 404 Strand .. .. Cb 7

Vauxhall Bridge, between Vauxhall and Millbank .. .. Ab 13

Vauxhall Park, South Lambeth Road, 8 acres in extent .. .. Ac 13

Victoria and Albert Museum, South Kensington. Open daily from 10-10, free on Mondays, Tuesdays, and Saturdays; other days from 10 to 4, 5, or 6, on payment of 6d.; Sundays, 2-5, free .. .. Cd 11

Victoria Bridge, between Pimlico and Battersea Park .. .. Da 12

Victoria Dock, Canning Town. Area 74 acres, and a tidal basin of 16 acres Ba 15

Victoria Embankment, Opened in 1870, and cost nearly £2,000,000 .. Cc 7

Victoria Park, 217 acres in extent, one of the finest parks in London .. Dc 9

Vintners' Hall, Upper Thames Street. Built by Wren in 1671 .. Bc 6

Virginia Water, Surrey, 23 m. by S. W. Ry. from Waterloo. An artificial lake, with very pleasing views, formed by the Duke of Cumberland in the year after Culloden .. .. Ab 18

Waldorf Theatre, Aldwych .. .. Db 7

Wallace Collection, Hertford House, Manchester Square. Open free on Mon. from 2 p.m., Wed., Thur., and Sat., from 10 a.m. to 4-5, or 6 p.m.; Tues. and Fri. from 11 a.m., 6d.; Sundays from 2 p.m. during summer Ac 8

Walton-on-Thames, 17 miles from London by the S.W. Railway .. Bc 18

Waltham Abbey, 13 Miles from Liverpool Street. It was founded by Harold in 1066, and contains some very early Norman architecture .. Ba 5

Wandsworth Bridge, connects Wandsworth with Fulham .. .. Cc 12

Wandsworth Common, between Clapham and Wimbledon .. .. Ab 16

War Office, Whitehall. Hours, 10-5 .. .. Cc 7

Waterloo Bridge.—Built by Rennie in 1811-17. Cost £1,000,000. Quite the finest bridge over the Thames, and said by Canova, the Italian sculptor, to be worth a journey from Italy to see it .. .. Db 7

Waterlow Park. Presented to the public in 1891 by Sir Sydney Waterlow

Watling Street, City. Is a part of the old Roman road from Dover to Chester .. .. Bc 6

Wax Chandler's Hall, Gresham Street .. .. Bb 6

Wellington Barracks, Birdcage Walk .. .. Bc 7

Wellington Statue, Hyde Park Corner .. .. Dc 11

Welsh Harp, Hendon, 5½ m. from St Pancras or King's Cross (Metr.) .. Ca 18

Plate No.

Wembly Park, near Harrow, by rail from Baker Street .. .. Ca 13
Wesleyan Methodist Hall, Tothill Street .. .. Cc 7
Wesley's Chapel and Museum, Bunhill Fields .. .. .. Ba 6
West Brompton and Stamford Bridge Grounds.—Sports, etc. .. Bb 12
West India Docks, between Limehouse and Blackwall. Area, including
    Blackwall Basin and South Dock Basin, 92¾ acres .. .. .. Cc 14
West London Theatre, 69 Church Street, Edgware Road .. .. Cb 11
Westbourne Park Baptist Chapel, Westbourne Grove .. .. Bb 11
Westminster Abbey.—Free ; nave and cloistsrs, 6d. (except Mon. & Tues.) Cc 7
Westminster Bridge, built in 1856-62, at a cost of £250,000 .. .. Cc 7
Westminster Column. Erected to commemorate former pupils of West-
    minster School who fell in the Crimea or the Indian Mutiny .. Cc 7
Westminster Hall. Begun by William Rufus in 1097, almost destroyed
    by fire in 1291, remodelled and enlarged by Richard II. in 1398. One of
    the largest halls in the world, with a ceiling unsupported by columns, its
    length is 290 feet, breadth 68, and height 92 .. .. Cc 7
Westminster Hospital, Broad Sanctuary .. .. Cc 7
Westminster R. C. Cathedral, Foundation stone laid June 1895 .. Bd 7
Westminster School, Dean's Yard, Westminster .. .. .. Cd 7
Whitefield's Tabernacle, Tottenham Court Road .. .. .. Bc 8
White Lodge, Richmond Park .. .. Bb 17
Whitehall Chapel. Given by Queen Victoria in 1893 to the United
    Service Institution for a museum of National treasures connected with
    Army and Navy ; daily, 6d. .. .. Cc 7
Wimbledon Common. Until 1889 the annual meeting place of the
    National Rifle Association. 8 m. by rail from Waterloo, Ludgate Hill,
    London Bridge, or Victoria .. .. Cb 17
Windsor Castle. 22 m. from Paddington or Waterloo Stations. Admis-
    sion during the king's absence only, on Tuesdays. Wednesdays, and
    Thursdays ; Tuesdays and Thursdays ; Adults 1/-, children 6d. .. Ab 18
Woolwich.—The chief feature of Woolwich is the arsenal, one of the most
    extensive and complete establishments of its kind in the world. The
    The arsenal was transferred from Moorfields to Woolwich in 1716. The
    dockyard dates from the reign of Henry VIII. Admission to the Arsenal
    on Tuesdays and Thursdays, 10 and 11.30 a.m., 2 and 4.30 p.m. Tickets
    obtainable at the War Office .. .. Cb 15
Woolwich Common.—Military exercises and reviews are held on Wool-
    wich Common ; and at the practice range, on the marshes to the east
    all cannon and new inventions in artillery are proved .. .. Cb 15
Wormwood Scrubbs, near Notting Hill. A convict prison stands on
    part of the common .. .. Ab 11
Wyndham's Theatre, Cranbourne Street .. .. Cb 7
Zoological Gardens, Regent's Park. Admission 1/- ; on Mondays, 6d. ;
    on Sundays only by order from a member .. .. Aa 8

Albert Hall.

HOTELS.

Plate No.

Adelphi, 1 John Street	Cb 7		Horseshoe, 264 Tottenham Court Road	Cc 8
Albemarle, 1 Albemarle Street	Bb 7		Hotel Continental Regent St., S.W.	Bb 7
Albion, 172 Aldersgate Street	Bb 6		Howard, Norfolk Street, Strand	Db 7
Alexandra, St George's Pl., Hyde-Pk.	Ac 7		Hyde Park, Albert Gate	Dc 11
Andertons, 162 Fleet Street	Ea 7		Inn's of Court, High Holborn	Dc 8
Angus's, New Bridge Street, E.C.,	Ac 6		Ivanhoe, Bloomsbury Street	Cc 8
Armfields, South Place, Finsbury	Bb 6		Kenilworth, Great Russell Street	Cc 8
Arundel, Arundel Street, Strand	Db 7		Kingsley, Hart Street, Bloomsbury	Cc 8
Bailey's, Gloucester Road Station	Cd 11		Klein's, 38 Finsbury Square	Cb 6
Bedford, Southampton Row	Cc 8		Langham, Portland Place	Bc 7
Bedford Head, 235 Tottenham Co. Rd.	Cc 8		Limmer's, George Street, Hanover Sq.	Bb 7
Berkeley, Berkeley Street	Bd 7		Long's, New Bond Street	Bb 7
Berner's, Berner's Street	Bc 8		Loudoun, Surrey Street, Strand	Db 7
Bolton Mansions, Bolton Gardens	Ca 12		Manchester, 136 Aldersgate Street	Bb 6
Bridge House, 4 Borough High Street	Bb 6		Metropole, Northumberland Avenue	Cb 7
Brown's, Dover Street	Bb 7		Midland Grand, St Pancras Station	Ca 8
Brunswick, Jermyn Street	Ba 7		Morley's, Trafalgar Square	Cb 7
Buecker's, Christopher St., Finsbury Sq.	Ca 6		Norfolk, Harrington Road	Cd 11
Buckingham (Tp.), Buck'ham St., Strand	Cb 7		Norfolk, Surrey Street	Db 7
Buckingham Palace, Buckingham Gate	Bc 7		Park, Park Place, St James Street	Bc 7
Bucklands, Brook St., Grosvenor Sq.	Ab 7		Portland, 97 Great Portland Street	Bc 8
Burlington, 19 Cork Street, Bond St.	Bb 7		Prince of Wales, De Vere Gars., Kens.	Cc 11
Cadogan, 75 Sloane Street	Da 12		Princes', Jermyn Street	Bb 7
Caledonian, Adelphi Terrace	Cb 7		Queen's, Leicester Square	Cb 7
Cannon Street, at Railway Station	Bc 6		Royal, (De Keyser's) Victoria Embank.	Eb 7
Carlton, Pall Mall	Bc 7		Royal Palace, Kensington High Street	Bc 11
Castle and Falcon, Aldersgate Street	Bb 6		Russell, Russell Square	Cb 8
Cecil, Strand	Cb 7		Sackville, 28 Sackville Street	Bb 7
Charing Cross, at Railway Station	Cb 7		St Ermin's, Caxton St., Westminster	Bd 7
Claridge's, Brook St., Grosvenor Sq.	Ab 7		Salisbury, Salisbury Square, Fleet St.	Eb 7
Cockburn House, 9 Endsleigh Gardens	Cb 8		Savoy, Victoria Embankment	Db 7
Covent Garden, Southampton Street	Cb 7		South Kensington, Queen's Gate Terr.	Cc 11
Curzon, Curzon Street, Mayfair	Ab 7		Suttie's, (Temp.) 26 Bedford Place,	
De Vere, De Vere Gars., Kensington	Cc 11		Russell Square	Cc 8
Dieudonne, 11 Ryder Street (French)	Bb 7		Tavistock, Covent Garden	Cb 7
Devonshire House, 12 Bishopsgate St.	Cb 6		Temple, Arundel Street, Strand	Db 7
Esmond, Montague Street, Russell Sq.	Cc 8		Thackeray, Gt. Russell St., Bloomsbury	Cc 8
Euston, Euston Station	Bb 8		Three Nuns, Aldgate	Cc 6
First Avenue, High Holborn	Dc 8		Tranter's (Temp.) 6-9 Bridgewater Sq.	Ba 6
Freemason's Tavern, Great Queen St.	Dc 8		Tudor, Oxford Street	Bc 8
Golden Cross, Charing Cross	Cb 7		Victoria, Northumberland Avenue	Cb 7
Grand, Northumberland Avenue	Cb 7		Waverley, 37 King Street, Cheapside	Bc 6
Gt. Central, Marylebone Station	Cb 11		Waverley, Southampton Row, Russell Sq.	Cb 8
Gt. Eastern, Liverpool Street	Cb 6		West Central (Temp.), Southampton	
Gt. Northern, King's Cross Station	Ca 8		Row	Cc 8
Gt. Western, Paddington Station	Cb 11		Westminster Palace, Victoria Street	Cd 7
Grosvenor, Victoria Station	Ad 7		Wild's (Temp.), 70 Euston Square	Bb 8
Hans Crescent, Hans Cres., Sloane St.	Dd 11		Wild's (Temp.), 30 Ludgate Hill	Ab 6
Haxell's, 369 Strand	Db 7		Wilton, Victoria Station	Bd 7
Holborn Viaduct, at Station	Ec 8		Windsor, Victoria Street, Westminster	Bd 7
Horrex's, Norfolk Street, Strand	Db 7		York, 9 Albemarle Street	Bb 7

RESTAURANTS.

Adelphi, (Gatti), Strand	Cb 7		Kettner's, 28-31 Church Street, Soho	Cb 7
Auction Mart, Tokenhouse Yard	Bb 6		Lake's, 49 Cheapside	Bb 6
Blanchard's, 1-7 Beak St., Regent St.	Bb 7		London Tavern, 53 Fenchurch Street	Cc 6
Blue Posts, 14 Rupert Street. Oysters	Cb 7		Monico's, 19 Shaftesbury Avenue	Bb 7
Burlington, 169 Regent Street	Bb 7		Monte Carlo, 2 Leicester Street	Cb 7
Cafe Restaurant de Paris, 74 Ludgate			Old Cheshire Cheese, Wine Office Co.	Ea 7
Hill	Ab 6		Pagani's, 44 Great Portland Street	Bc 8
Cafe Royal, 68 Regent Street	Bb 7		Pall Mall, 9 Haymarket	Cb 7
Carr's, 265 Strand	Db 7		Pimm's, 3 Poultry. Oysters	Bc 6
Cavour's, 20 Leicester Square	Cb 7		Prince's Hall, Piccadilly	Bb 7
Cock, 22 Fleet Street	Db 7		Rainbow, 15 Fleet Street	Db 7
Corn Exchange, 58 Mark Lane	Cc 6		Romano's, 399 Strand	Db 7
Criterion, Piccadilly Circus	Bb 7		St James', 69 Regent Street	Bb 7
Crosby Hall, Bishopsgate Street	Cb 6		Scott's, 18 Coventry Street. Oysters	Cb 7
Daniel Lambert, Ludgate Hill	Ab 6		Ship, 45 Charing Cross	Cb 7
Epitaux's, 9 Haymarket	Cb 7		Ship & Turtle, 129 Leadenhall Street	Cc 6
Formaggia's, 109 Regent Street	Bb 7		Simpson's, 101-103 Strand	Cb 7
Frascati's, 26-32 Oxford Street	Cc 8		Slater's, 212 Piccadilly	Bb 7
Gaiety, Strand	Db 7		Sweeting's, 158 Cheapside. Fish	Bb 6
Gatti's, 436 Strand	Cb 7		Spiers & Ponds Buffet, Holborn Via-	
Guildhall, 81-83 Gresham Street	Bb 6		duct Station	Ec 8
Hatchetts', 67a Piccadilly	Bb 7		Three Tuns, Billingsgate Market	Cc 6
Holborn, 218 High Holborn	Dc 8		Trocadero, Shaftesbury Avenue	Bb 7
Horseshoe, 267 Tottenham Court Road	Cc 7		Willis's, 26 King Street, St James's	Bc 8

CAB FARES.

FARES TO OR FROM	Bank, Threadneedle Street.	Broad Street.	Cannon Street.	Charing Cross.	Euston.	Fenchurch St.	King's Cross.	Liverpool St.	London Bridge.	Marylebone.	Paddington.	St Pancras.	Victoria Term.	Waterloo.
Agricultural Hall, Islington	1/0	1/0	1/6	1/6	1/0	1/6	1/0	1/0	1/6	1/6	2/0	1/0	2/0	1/6
Albert Hall, Kensington	2/6	2/6	2/6	1/6	2/0	2/6	2/0	2/6	2/6	1/6	1/0	2/0	1/0	2/0
Bank of England, Threadneedle Street	—	1/0	1/0	1/0	1/6	1/0	1/6	1/0	1/0	2/0	2/6	1/6	2/0	1/0
Bayswater Road, Lancaster Gate	2/6	2/6	2/6	1/6	1/6	2/6	2/0	2/6	2/6	1/0	1/0	1/6	1/6	2/0
Bishopsgate Street, Houndsditch	1/0	1/0	1/0	1/6	1/6	1/0	1/6	1/0	1/0	2/6	2/6	1/6	2/0	1/0
Blackfriars Road, Charlotte Street	1/0	1/0	1/0	1/0	1/6	1/0	1/6	1/0	1/0	2/0	2/0	1/6	1/6	1/0
Bloomsbury Square, any part	1/0	1/6	1/0	1/0	1/0	1/6	1/0	1/6	1/6	1/6	1/6	1/0	1/6	1/0
Bond Street (New), Oxford Street	1/6	1/6	1/6	1/0	1/0	2/0	1/0	2/0	2/0	1/0	1/0	1/0	1/0	1/6
Botanic Gardens, Regent's Park	2/0	2/0	2/0	1/6	1/0	2/0	1/0	2/0	2/0	1/0	1/0	1/0	1/6	1/6
Bow Street Police Court	1/0	1/6	1/0	1/0	1/0	1/6	1/0	1/6	1/0	1/6	1/6	1/0	1/0	1/0
British Museum	1/0	1/6	1/0	1/0	1/0	1/6	1/0	1/6	1/6	1/6	1/6	1/0	1/6	1/0
Bryanston Square, any part	2/0	2/0	2/0	1/6	1/0	2/0	1/6	2/6	2/6	1/0	1/0	1/6	1/0	1/0
Buckingham Gate, St James's Park	1/6	2/0	1/6	1/0	1/6	2/0	1/6	2/0	1/6	1/6	1/6	1/6	1/0	1/0
Camberwell, St Giles's Church	2/0	2/0	2/0	2/0	2/6	2/0	2/6	2/0	1/6	3/0	3/0	2/6	2/0	1/6
Camberwell Green, Denmark Hill	2/0	2/0	2/0	2/0	2/6	2/0	2/6	2/0	1/6	3/0	3/0	2/6	1/6	1/6
Camden Town, Mother Red Cap	2/0	2/0	2/0	1/6	1/0	2/0	1/0	2/0	2/0	1/6	1/6	1/0	2/0	1/6
Cattle Market, Metropolitan (S.E. corn.)	2/0	2/0	2/0	2/0	1/0	2/0	1/0	2/0	2/0	2/0	2/0	1/0	2/6	2/0
Cavendish Square, any part	1/6	2/0	1/6	1/0	1/0	2/0	1/0	2/0	2/0	1/0	1/0	1/0	1/0	1/6
Charing Cross, King Charles's Statute	1/0	1/6	1/0	1/0	1/0	1/6	1/6	1/6	1/6	1/6	1/6	1/0	1/0	1/0
Chelsea Hospital, Chapel Entrance	2/0	2/6	2/0	1/6	2/0	2/6	2/6	2/6	2/0	1/6	1/6	2/6	1/0	1/6
Chelsea Town Hall	2/6	2/6	2/6	1/6	2/6	2/6	2/6	2/6	2/6	1/6	1/6	2/6	1/0	1/6
Clapham Common, The Plough	2/6	2/6	2/6	2/0	3/0	2/6	3/0	2/6	2/0	2/6	3/0	3/0	1/6	2/0
Cromwell Road, Collingham Road	2/6	3/0	2/6	2/0	2/6	3/0	2/6	3/0	2/6	1/6	1/6	2/6	1/6	2/0
Custom House, Thames Street	1/0	1/0	1/0	1/6	1/6	1/0	1/6	1/0	1/0	2/6	2/6	1/6	2/0	1/0
De Vere Gardens, Kensington Road	2/6	2/6	2/6	1/6	2/0	2/6	2/6	2/6	2/6	1/6	1/0	2/0	1/6	2/0
Downing Street, Treasury Passage	1/6	1/6	1/6	1/0	1/6	1/6	1/6	1/6	1/6	1/6	1/6	1/6	1/0	1/0
Earl's Court Exhibition, Warwick Road	3/0	3/0	3/0	2/0	2/6	3/0	3/0	3/0	3/0	2/0	1/6	2/6	1/6	2/6
Eaton Square, The Church	2/0	2/0	2/0	1/0	2/0	2/0	2/0	2/0	2/0	1/6	1/6	2/0	1/0	1/0
Egyptian Hall, Piccadilly	1/6	1/6	1/6	1/0	1/0	1/6	1/6	1/6	1/6	1/0	1/6	1/0	1/0	1/0
Elephant and Castle, Newington	1/0	1/0	1/0	1/0	2/0	1/0	1/6	1/0	1/0	2/0	2/6	2/0	1/6	1/0
Ennismore Gardens, Kensington Gore	2/0	2/6	2/0	1/6	2/0	2/6	2/0	2/6	2/0	1/0	1/0	2/0	1/0	1/6
Finsbury Square, any part	1/0	1/0	1/0	1/6	1/6	1/0	1/6	1/0	1/0	2/0	2/6	1/6	2/0	1/6
Fitzroy Square, any part	1/6	1/6	1/6	1/0	1/0	2/0	1/0	2/0	2/0	1/0	1/0	1/0	1/6	1/6
Fleet Street, Fetter Lane	1/0	1/0	1/0	1/0	1/0	1/0	1/0	1/0	1/0	1/6	2/0	1/0	1/6	1/0
Fulham Road, West London Cemetery	3/0	3/0	3/0	2/0	2/6	3/0	3/0	3/0	3/0	2/0	1/6	2/6	1/6	2/0
General Post Office	1/0	1/0	1/0	1/0	1/6	1/0	1/0	1/0	1/0	2/0	2/0	1/0	1/6	1/0
Great Marlborough Street Police Court	1/6	1/6	1/6	1/0	1/0	1/6	1/0	1/6	1/6	1/0	1/0	1/0	1/0	1/0
Grosvenor Road, Tate Gallery	1/6	2/0	1/6	1/0	1/6	1/6	2/0	2/0	1/6	2/0	2/0	2/0	1/0	1/0
Grosvenor Square, any part	2/0	2/0	2/0	1/0	1/0	2/0	1/6	2/0	2/0	1/0	1/0	1/6	1/0	1/6
Guildhall, City	1/0	1/0	1/0	1/0	1/6	1/0	1/6	1/0	1/0	2/0	2/6	1/6	2/0	1/0
Hackney, Well Street, Mare Street	1/6	1/6	1/6	2/6	2/6	1/6	2/0	1/6	2/0	3/0	3/6	2/0	3/0	2/6
Hanover Square, any part	1/6	1/6	1/6	1/0	1/0	2/0	1/0	2/0	2/0	1/0	1/0	1/0	1/0	1/6
Harley Street, Devonshire Street	1/6	2/0	2/0	1/0	1/0	2/0	1/0	2/0	2/0	1/0	1/0	1/0	1/6	1/6
High Holborn, Chancery Lane	1/0	1/0	1/0	1/0	1/0	1/0	1/0	1/0	1/0	1/6	1/6	1/0	1/6	1/0
HOSPITALS—														
Guy's, High Street, Borough	1/0	1/0	1/0	1/6	2/0	1/0	1/6	1/0	1/0	2/6	2/6	1/6	1/6	1/0
King's College, 7 Portugal Street	1/0	1/0	1/0	1/0	1/0	1/0	1/0	1/0	1/0	1/6	1/6	1/0	1/6	1/0
London, Whitechapel Road	1/0	1/0	1/0	2/0	2/0	1/0	2/0	1/0	1/0	3/0	3/0	2/0	2/6	1/6
London Fever, L'pool Rd., Islington	1/6	1/0	1/6	1/6	1/0	1/6	1/0	1/6	1/6	1/6	2/0	1/0	2/0	1/6
Middlesex, Mortimer Street	1/6	1/6	1/6	1/0	1/0	1/6	1/0	1/6	1/6	1/0	1/0	1/0	1/6	1/0
Royal Free, Gray's Inn Road	1/0	1/0	1/0	1/0	1/0	1/6	1/0	1/6	1/6	1/6	1/6	1/0	2/0	1/6
St Bartholomew's, Smithfield	1/0	1/0	1/0	1/0	1/6	1/0	1/0	1/0	1/0	2/0	2/0	1/0	1/6	1/0
St Thomas's, Westminster Bridge	1/0	1/6	1/0	1/0	1/6	1/6	1/6	1/6	1/0	2/0	2/0	1/6	1/0	1/0
University, Gower Street	1/6	1/6	1/6	1/0	1/0	1/6	1/0	1/6	2/0	1/0	1/6	1/0	1/6	1/0
HOTELS—														
Albemarle	1/6	1/6	1/6	1/0	1/6	1/6	1/6	1/6	1/6	1/0	1/0	1/6	1/0	1/0
Carlton	1/6	1/6	1/6	1/0	1/0	1/6	1/6	1/6	1/6	1/0	1/6	1/6	1/0	1/0
Cecil, Strand	1/0	1/6	1/0	1/0	1/0	1/6	1/6	1/6	1/6	1/6	1/6	1/0	1/0	1/0
Grand	1/0	1/6	1/0	1/0	1/0	1/6	1/0	1/6	1/6	1/6	1/6	1/0	1/0	1/0
Metropole	1/0	1/6	1/0	1/0	1/0	1/6	1/6	1/6	1/6	1/6	1/6	1/0	1/0	1/0
Houses of Parliament	1/6	1/6	1/6	1/0	1/6	1/6	1/6	1/6	1/6	1/6	2/0	1/6	1/0	1/0
Hyde Park Corner, St George's Hosp.	2/0	2/0	2/0	1/0	1/6	2/0	1/6	2/0	2/0	1/0	1/0	1/6	1/0	1/6

Cab Fares

FARES TO AND FROM	Bank, Threadneedle Street.	Broad Street.	Cannon Street,	Charing Cross.	Euston.	Fenchurch St.	King's Cross.	Liverpool St.	London Bridge.	Marylebone.	Paddington.	St Pancras.	Victoria Term.	Waterloo.
Imperial Institute	2/6	2/6	2/0	1/6	2/0	2/6	2/0	2/6	2/6	1/6	1/0	2/0	1/0	2/0
Kennington Oval	1/6	2/0	1/6	1/6	2/0	1/6	2/0	2/0	1/6	2/0	2/6	2/0	1/0	1/0
Lincoln's Inn Fields, Serle Street	1/0	1/0	1/0	1/0	1/0	1/0	1/0	1/0	1/0	1/6	2/0	1/0	1/6	1/0
London Docks	1/0	1/0	1/0	1/6	2/0	1/0	2/0	1/0	1/0	2/6	3/0	2/0	2/0	1/6
Lord's Cricket Ground	2/6	2/6	2/6	2/0	1/6	2/6	1/6	2/6	2/6	1/0	1/0	1/6	1/6	2/0
Ludgate Circus	1/0	1/0	1/0	1/0	1/0	1/0	1/0	1/0	1/0	2/0	2/0	1/0	1/6	1/0
Madame Tussaud's, Baker Street	2/0	2/0	2/0	1/6	1/0	2/0	1/0	2/0	2/0	1/0	1/0	1/0	1/0	1/6
Mansion House, City	1/0	1/0	1/0	1/0	1/6	1/0	1/6	1/0	1/0	2/0	2/6	1/6	2/0	1/0
Marble Arch, Bayswater Road	2/0	2/0	2/0	1/0	1/0	2/0	1/6	2/0	2/0	1/0	1/0	1/6	1/0	1/6
Marylebone Police Court	2/0	2/6	2/0	1/6	1/0	2/6	1/6	2/6	2/6	1/0	1/0	1/0	1/6	2/0
Mint, Tower Hill	1/0	1/0	1/0	1/6	2/0	1/0	1/6	1/0	1/0	2/6	2/6	2/0	2/0	1/6
National Gallery	1/0	1/6	1/0	1/0	1/0	1/6	1/6	1/6	1/6	1/6	2/6	1/0	1/0	1/0
Natural History Museum	2/6	2/6	2/6	1/6	2/0	2/6	2/6	2/6	2/6	1/6	1/0	2/6	1/0	2/0
New Scotland Yard	1/0	1/6	1/0	1/0	1/6	1/6	1/6	1/6	1/0	1/6	2/0	1/6	1/0	1/0
Old Bailey, Central Criminal Court	1/0	1/0	1/0	1/0	1/0	1/0	1/0	1/0	1/0	2/0	2/0	1/0	1/6	1/0
Old Broad Street, Gt. Winchester St	1/0	1/0	1/0	1/6	1/6	1/0	1/6	1/0	1/0	2/6	2/6	1/6	2/0	1/0
Oxford Street, Regent Circus	1/6	1/6	1/6	1/0	1/0	1/6	1/0	1/6	1/6	1/0	1/0	1/0	1/0	1/0
Oxford Street, Tottenham Court Road	1/0	1/6	1/6	1/0	1/0	1/6	1/0	1/6	1/6	1/0	1/6	1/0	1/6	1/0
Pall Mall, War Office	1/6	1/6	1/6	1/0	1/6	1/6	1/6	1/6	1/6	1/6	1/6	1/6	1/0	1/0
Peckham, High Street, Rye Lane	2/0	2/0	2/0	2/6	3/0	2/0	3/0	2/0	1/6	3/6	3/6	3/0	2/0	2/0
Piccadilly, Half-Moon Street	1/6	2/0	1/6	1/0	1/6	2/0	1/6	2/0	2/0	1/0	1/0	1/6	1/0	1/0
Portland Place, Weymouth Street	1/6	2/0	1/6	1/0	1/0	2/0	1/0	2/0	2/0	1/0	1/0	1/0	1/6	1/6
STATIONS—														
Charing Cross	1/0	1/6	1/0	—	1/0	1/6	1/6	1/6	1/6	1/6	1/6	1/0	1/0	1/0
Euston	1/6	1/6	1/6	1/0	—	1/6	1/0	2/0	2/0	1/0	1/6	1/0	2/0	1/6
Fenchurch Street	1/0	1/0	1/0	1/6	1/6	—	1/6	1/0	1/0	2/6	2/6	1/6	2/0	1/6
King's Cross	1/6	1/6	1/6	1/6	1/0	1/6	—	1/6	1/6	1/6	1/6	1/0	2/0	1/6
Liverpool Street	1/0	1/0	1/0	1/6	1/6	1/0	1/6	—	1/0	2/6	2/6	1/6	2/0	1/6
London Bridge	1/0	1/0	1/0	1/6	2/0	1/0	1/6	1/0	—	2/6	2/6	1/6	1/6	1/0
Ludgate Hill	1/0	1/0	1/0	1/0	1/0	1/0	1/0	1/0	1/0	2/0	2/0	1/0	1/6	1/0
Marylebone	2/0	2/6	2/0	1/6	1/0	2/6	1/6	2/6	2/6	—	1/0	1/0	1/6	2/0
Moorgate Street	1/0	1/0	1/0	1/6	1/6	1/0	1/6	1/0	1/0	2/0	2/6	1/6	2/0	1/0
Paddington	2/6	2/6	2/6	1/6	1/6	2/6	1/6	2/6	2/6	1/0	—	1/6	1/6	2/0
St Pancras	1/6	1/6	1/6	1/0	1/0	1/6	1/0	1/6	1/6	1/0	1/6	—	2/0	1/6
Victoria Terminus	2/0	2/0	2/0	1/0	2/0	2/0	2/0	2/0	1/6	1/6	1/6	2/0	—	1/0
Waterloo	1/0	1/6	1/0	1/0	1/6	1/0	1/6	1/6	1/6	1/6	2/0	2/0	1/0	—
Russell Square	1/0	1/6	1/6	1/0	1/0	1/6	1/0	1/6	1/6	1/6	1/6	1/0	1/6	1/0
St James's Square	1/6	1/6	1/6	1/0	1/0	1/6	1/6	1/6	1/6	1/6	1/6	1/6	1/0	1/0
St Katharine's Docks	1/0	1/0	1/0	1/6	2/0	1/0	2/0	1/0	1/0	2/6	3/0	2/0	2/6	1/6
St Paul's Cathedral	1/0	1/0	1/0	1/0	1/6	1/0	1/0	1/0	1/0	2/0	2/0	1/0	1/6	1/0
Sloane Square, Sloane Street	2/0	2/6	2/0	1/6	2/0	2/6	2/0	2/6	2/0	1/6	1/6	2/0	1/0	1/6
Smithfield (West), Long Lane	1/0	1/0	1/0	1/0	1/6	1/0	1/0	1/0	1/0	2/0	2/0	1/0	1/6	1/0
Soho Square, any part	1/6	1/6	1/6	1/0	1/0	1/6	1/0	1/6	1/6	1/0	1/6	1/0	1/0	1/0
Strand, Law Courts	1/0	1/0	1/0	1/0	1/0	1/0	1/0	1/0	1/0	1/6	2/0	1/0	1/6	1/0
THEATRES—														
Adelphi	1/0	1/6	1/0	1/0	1/0	1/6	1/0	1/6	1/0	1/6	1/6	1/0	1/0	1/0
Alhambra, Leicester Square	1/0	1/6	1/0	1/0	1/0	1/6	1/0	1/6	1/0	1/6	1/6	1/0	1/0	1/0
Court, Sloane Square	2/0	2/6	2/0	1/6	2/0	2/6	2/0	2/6	2/0	1/6	1/6	2/0	1/0	1/6
Drury Lane	1/0	1/0	1/0	1/0	1/0	1/0	1/0	1/6	1/6	1/6	1/6	1/0	1/0	1/0
Gaiety	1/0	1/0	1/0	1/0	1/0	1/0	1/0	1/0	1/0	1/6	1/6	1/0	1/0	1/0
Garrick	1/0	1/6	1/0	1/0	1/0	1/6	1/0	1/6	1/6	1/6	1/6	1/0	1/0	1/0
Globe	1/0	1/0	1/0	1/0	1/0	1/0	1/0	1/0	1/0	1/6	1/6	1/0	1/6	1/0
Grand, Islington	1/0	1/0	1/0	1/6	1/0	1/6	1/0	1/6	1/6	1/6	2/0	1/0	2/0	1/6
Haymarket	1/6	1/6	1/6	1/0	1/0	1/6	1/0	1/6	1/6	1/6	1/6	1/6	1/0	1/0
Lyceum, Wellington Street, Strand	1/0	1/0	1/0	1/0	1/0	1/0	1/0	1/0	1/0	1/6	1/6	1/0	1/0	1/0
Lyric	1/6	1/6	1/6	1/0	1/0	1/6	1/0	1/6	1/6	1/6	1/6	1/6	1/0	1/0
Olympia, Hammersmith	3/0	3/6	3/0	2/6	2/6	3/6	3/0	3/6	3/0	2/0	1/6	3/0	2/0	2/6
Palace, Shaftsbury Avenue	1/0	1/6	1/6	1/0	1/0	1/6	1/0	1/6	1/6	1/6	1/6	1/0	1/0	1/0
Princess's, Oxford Street	1/6	1/6	1/6	1/0	1/0	1/6	1/0	1/6	1/6	1/0	1/0	1/0	1/0	1/0
Royalty, Soho	1/6	1/6	1/6	1/0	1/0	1/6	1/0	1/6	1/6	1/0	1/6	1/0	1/0	1/0
Wyndham's	1/0	1/6	1/0	1/0	1/0	1/6	1/0	1/6	1/6	1/6	1/6	1/0	1/0	1/0
Zoological Gardens, Regent's Park	2/0	2/6	2/6	1/6	1/0	2/6	1/0	2/6	2/6	1/0	1/6	1/0	2/0	2/0

Tower Bridge.

40

No. 1.—Acton and Ealing *via* Ealing Common.

No. 2.—Acton to Charing Cross—*Red*—*Via* Uxbridge Road, Notting Hill, Marble Arch, Oxford Street, Regent Street, and Pall Mall East.

No. 3.—Baker Street to Charing Cross—*Light Green*—*Via* Baker Street, Wigmore Street Marylebone Lane, Nottingham Place, Cavendish Street, Regent Street, and Pall Mall.

No. 4.—Baker Street Station to Piccadilly Circus—*Brown*—*Via* Baker Street, Portman Square Oxford Street, Bond Street, and Piccadilly.

No. 5.—Baker Street Station to Victoria Station—*Brown*—*Via* Baker Street Portman Square Oxford Street, North and South Audley Streets, Park Lane, and Grosvenor Place.

No. 6.—Barnsbury to Kennington Park—*Brown*—*Via* Thornhill Rd., Liverpool Rd., "Angel,' Goswell Road, Aldersgate Street, Ludgate Hill, Blackfriars Bridge, and "Elephant and Castle."

No. 7.—Battersea Park to Knightsbridge—*Brown*—*Via* Victoria Bridge and Sloane Street.

No. 8.—Battersea Pk. to S. Hackney—*Chocolate*—*Via* Battersea Pk. Rd., Cheyne Walk, King's Rd., Sloane St., Piccadilly Circus, Regent St., Pall Mall, Charing Cross, Strand, Fleet St., Ludgate Circus, Cannon St., Queen Victoria St., Liverpool St., Shoreditch, High St., Bethnal Green Road, Cambridge Road, Victoria Park Road.

No. 9.—Battersea Pk. to Victoria Sta.—*Brown*—*Via* Victoria Br. and Buckingham Pal. Rd.

No. 10.—Bayswater to Shoreditch Church—*Dark Green*—From "Clarendon," *via* Elgin Crescent, Kensington Park Road, Westbourne Grove, Praed Street, Edgware Road, Oxford Street, Holborn, Cheapside, Liverpool Street, and Norton Folgate.

No. 11.—Bayswater (Ledbury Road) to Victoria—*Red*—Westbourne Grove, Praed Street, Edgware Road, Park Lane, Grosvenor Street.

No. 12.—Bermondsey to Gracechurch St.—*Light Green*—From "The Victory," Rotherhithe New Rd., *via* Southwark Park Rd., Grange Rd., Bermondsey St., Tooley St. and London Bridge.

No. 13.—Blackheath Station to Grove Park, *via* Lee.

No. 14.—Blackwall to Piccadilly Circus—*Blue*—*Via* East India Road, Commercial Road, Aldgate, Leadenhall Street, Queen Victoria Street, Fleet Street, Strand, and Haymarket.

No. 15.—Bow and Oxford Circus—*Green*—*Via* Bow Road, Whitechapel Road, Cornhill, Cheapside, Ludgate Hill, Fleet Street, Strand, Charing Cross, and Pall Mall East.

No. 16.—Brixton Church to Oxford Circus—*Green*—*Via* Brixton Road, Kennington Road, Westminster Bridge, Whitehall, Charing Cross, and Regent Street.

No. 17.—Brixton Hill to Gracechurch Street—*Green*—*Via* Brixton Road, Kennington Park Road, "Elephant and Castle," Borough, and London Bridge.

No. 18.—Camberwell—Camberwell Green to Magdala Hotel, Lordship Lane, Dulwich.

No. 19.—Camberwell to Camden Town—*Dark Blue*—*Via* Walworth Road, "Elephant and Castle," London Road, Waterloo Road, Strand, Charing Cross, Regent Street. Great Portland Street, and Albany Street, to "Britannia."

No. 20.—Camberwell Gate to Hackney Road—*Yellow*—*Via* Albany Road, Old Kent Road, Bermondsey, Tower Bridge Road, Tower Bridge, Minories, Commercial Street, Hackney Road.

No. 21.—Camberwell Gate to Hackney Road—*Yellow Via* Walworth Road, "Elephant and Castle," Cornhill and Shoreditch.

No. 22.—Camberwell Green to Clapham—*Green*—*Via* Denmark Hill, Coldharbour Lane, Acre Lane, Clapham Park Road, Clapham Common.

No. 23.—Camberwell Green to Cornhill—*Dark Green or Chocolate*—*Via* Walworth Road, "Elephant and Castle," Borough, London Bridge, Gracechurch Street.

No. 24.—Camberwell Green to King's Cross—*Blue*—*Via* Walworth Road, "Elephant and Castle," Waterloo Road, Strand, Chancery Lane, Holborn, Gray's Inn Road.

No. 25.—Camberwell Green to Victoria—*Green*—*Via* Camberwell New Rd., Kennington Oval, Vauxhall Bridge, and Vauxhall Bridge Road.

No. 26.—Camden Town to Charing Cross—*Yellow*—Same as 27 as far as Charing Cross, then *via* Whitehall and Victoria Street.

No. 27.—Camden Town to Waterloo Station, *via* Albany Street, Gt. Portland Street, Regent Street, Charing Cross, Strand, and Waterloo Bridge.

No. 28.—Camden Town to Victoria—*Yellow*—"Brecknock Arms," High St., Tottenham Court Rd., Oxford St., Charing Cross, Westminster, and Victoria Street.

No. 29.—Catford and Beckenham—Rushey Green, Catford, to Beckenham Junction Station, *via* Catford Bridge, Forest Hill, Sydenham, and High Street, Beckenham.

No. 30.—Catford to New Cross—*Green*—*Via* Lewisham High Road.

No. 31.—Catford to Sydenham—*Green*—*Via* Perry Vale.

No. 32.—Charing Cross to Child's Hill—*Blue and White*—*Via* Baker Street and Finchley Road.

No. 33.—Clapham Junction to Gracechurch Street—*Brown*—*Via* Lavender Hill, Wandsworth Rd., Vauxhall Rd., Albert Embankment, York Rd., Stamford St., Southwark St., & London Bridge.

No. 34.—Clapham Junction to Knightsbridge—*Blue*—*Via* Lavender Hill, Queen's Road, Battersea Park Road, Battersea Bridge, Lr. Sloane Street, and Sloane Street.

No. 35.—Cricklewood to Charing Cross—*Red*—From "The Crown," *via* Kilburn, Maida Vale, Edgware Road, Marble Arch, Oxford Street, Regent Street, and Pall Mall East.

No 36.—Deptford and City—Deptford to Gracechurch Street, *via* High Street, Deptford, Rotherhithe, Bermondsey, and London Bridge.

No. 37.—Deptford and Lewisham—Deptford Broadway to Lewisham, *via* Mill Lane.

No. 38.—Deptford and Poplar—*Via* Greenwich and Blackwall Tunnel.

No. 39.—Dulwich—"Lord Nelson," Old Kent Road to "Half Moon," Herne Hill, *via* High Street, Rye Lane, Peckham, Peckham Rye, and East Dulwich.

No. 40.—Ealing Broadway to Hanwell.

No. 41.—Ealing Sth. Sta. to Kew Br. Sta.—In connection with the Dist. & S. W. Railways.

No. 42.—Edgware Road Station to Gower Street Station—*Blue*—*Via* Edgware Road, Marble Arch, Oxford Street, Tottenham Court Road, and Euston Road.

Westminster Pier.

No. 43.—**"Elephant and Castle" to Clapton,** *via* London Br., Bishopsgate & Shoreditch.

No. 44.—**"Elephant and Castle" to Farringdon Road**—*Red*—*Via* London Road, Blackfriars Road, Blackfriars Bridge, Ludgate Circus, and Farringdon Street.

No. 45.—**"Elephant and Castle" to Earl's Court**—*Green*—*Via* Lr. & Up. Kennington La., Vauxhall Br., Buckingham Pal. Rd., Pimlico Rd., Sloane St., Brompton Rd., Cromwell Rd., Earl's Co.

No. 46.—**"Elephant and Castle" to Islington**—*Red*—*Via* Borough, London Bridge, King William Street, Bank, Cheapside. General Post Office, Aldersgate Street, and Goswell Road.

No. 47.—**"Elephant and Castle" to Vauxhall Station**—*Red*—*Via* Kennington Lane.

No. 48.—**"Elephant and Castle" to Stamford Hill**—*Light Green*—*Via* London Bridge, Bank, Bishopsgate, and Kingsland Road.

No. 49.—**Eltham**—Blackheath Station (S.E.R.) to Eltham, *via* Lee.

No. 50.—**Finsbury Park**—Finsbury Park Station (G.N.R.) to Lower Clapton, *via* Clissold Park.

No. 51.—**Fulham High Street and Liverpool Street**—*White*—*Via* "King's Head," Fulham High Street, Fulham Road, Broadway, Walham Green, Harwood Road, King's Road, Sloane Square, Lr. Sloane Street, Pimlico Road, Buckingham Palace Road, Victoria Station, Victoria St., Broad Sanctuary, Parliament Street, Whitehall, Charing Cross, Strand, Fleet St. and Ludgate Hill.

No. 52.—**Fulham and London Bridge Railways**—*White*—*Via* Salisbury Hotel, Dawes Rd., Walham Green, Fulham Rd., Brompton Rd., Hyde Park Corner, Piccadilly, Shaftesbury Av., Charing Cross Rd., New Oxford St., Holborn, Newgate St., General Post Office, Bank, King William St., Monument. Over London Bridge to Railway Station Yard.

No. 53.—**Fulham Palace Road and Oxford Circus**—*Brown*—*Via* "The Greyhound," Fulham Palace Rd., Lillie Rd., Richmond Rd., Old Brompton Rd., South Kensington Sta., Brompton Rd., Knightsbridge, Hyde Park Corner, Piccadilly, Regent St., to Oxford Circus.

No. 54.—**Fulham (Sand's End) to Old Ford**—*Brown*—"Hand and Flower," King's Road, Sloane Street, Piccadilly, Charing Cross, Fleet Street, Ludgate Hill, Cheapside, Bank, Threadneedle Street, Broad Street Bishopsgate Street, Bethnal Green Road.

No. 55.—**Fulham to Shoreditch**—*White*—From the "Salisbury Hotel," *via* Fulham Road, Walham Green, Brompton Rd., Sloane St., Piccadilly, Shaftesbury Av., Tottenham Co. Rd., New Oxford St., Holborn Viaduct, Cheapside, Bank, Threadneedle St., Bishopsgate, & Norton Folgate.

No. 56.—**Hackney Road**—Camberwell Green to Shoreditch Church, *via* Walworth Road, "Elephant and Castle," London Bridge, and Bishopsgate.

No. 57.—**Hammersmith to Barnes**—*Chocolate*—Hammersmith Broadway, Bridge Road, Hammersmith Bridge, Castelnau, Barnes Green, and "Bull's Head."

No. 58.—**Hammersmith to Caledonian Road**—*Red*—Broadway, Kensington, Knightsbridge, Piccadilly, Shaftesbury Avenue, Tottenham Court Rd., Euston Rd., King's Cross, Caledonian Rd.

No. 59.—**Hammersmith to Liverpool Street**—*Red*—Broadway, Kensington, Knightsbridge, Piccadilly, Charing Cross, Strand, Fleet St., Ludgate Hill, Cheapside, Moorgate St., London Wall.

No. 60.—**Hammersmith to Wandsworth**—*White and Green*—Broadway, Queen Street, Fulham Palace Road, Lillie Road, Dawes Road, Walham Green, Wandsworth Bridge, and High Street.

No. 61.—**Hampstead to Oxford Street**—*Yellow*—High Street, Haverstock Hill, Chalk Farm Road, "Britannia," Camden Town, Hampstead Road, Tottenham Court Road.

No. 62.—**Harlesden Green to Charing Cross**—*Red*—*via* Stonebridge Park, Kensal Green, Harrow Road, Praed Street, Edgware Road, Marble Arch, Oxford Street, Regent Street.

No. 63.—**Highbury to Green Lanes Chapel**—*Red*—*Via* Upper Street, Highbury Station, Highbury New Park.

No. 64.—**Highbury Station to Putney Bridge**—*Red*—*Via* Highbury New Park, "Angel," Rosebery Av., Theobald's Rd., Oxford St., Shaftesbury Av., Piccadilly, Sloane St., King's Rd, Parsons Green.

No. 65.—**Highgate to London Bridge Station**—*Dark Green*—Highbury, Holloway, Upper Street, "Angel," City Road, Moorgate Street, Bank, King William Street, and London Bridge.

No. 66.—**Highgate to Victoria**—*Yellow*—*Via* Archway Tavern, Junction Rd., Fortess Rd., Kentish Town Rd., Camden High St., Hampstead Rd., Tottenham Court Rd., Oxford St., Charing Cross Rd.

No. 67.—**Holloway to Bayswater**—*Chocolate*—Nag's Head, Holloway, *via* Camden Road. Park Street, Regent Park Street, Albert Road, St John's Wood Road, Clifton Gardens, Warwick Road, Harrow Road, Porchester Road, Queen's Road, Uxbridge Road.

No. 68.—**Holloway to W. Kensington**—*Dark Blue*—Nag's Head, Caledonian Rd., King's Cross, Euston Rd., Gt. Portland St., Regent St., Piccadilly, Knightsbridge, Old Brompton Rd., Lillie Rd.

No. 69.—**Hornsey Rise and Sloane Square**—*Dark Green*—*Via* Hornsey Rise, Hornsey Rd., Seven Sisters' Rd., Caledonian Rd., King's Cross, Marylebone Rd., Baker St., Oxford St., Park Lane, Hyde Park Corner, Sloane Street to "Star and Garter," Sloane Square.

No. 70.—**Hornsey to Victoria Station**—*Dark Green*—Shaftesbury Tavern, Hornsey Road, Seven Sisters' Road, Holloway Road, Upper Street, "Angel," St John's Street Road, Rosebery Avenue, Gray's Inn Road, Holborn, Chancery Lane, Strand, Charing Cross, Whitehall, Victoria Street.

No. 71.—**Islington to Newgate Street and West Smithfield**—*Red*—*Via* St John's Street Rd., Meat Market, Giltspur Street, and St Sepulchre's Church.

No. 72.—**Kennington Park and Baker Street Station**—*Green*—*Via* Kennington Park Road, London Road, Blackfriars Rd., St Bride's St., Holborn, Gray's Inn Road, King's Cross, Euston Rd.

No. 73.—**Kennington Park to Oxford Circus**—*Red*—*Via* Kennington Road. Westminster Bridge Road, Parliament Street, Pall Mall East, Piccadilly Circus, Oxford Circus.

No. 74.—**Kensal Green to London Br.**—*Yellow*—*Via* Harrow Rd., Porchester Rd., Bishop's Rd., Harrow Rd., Edgware Rd., Oxford St., Holborn, Cheapside, Bank, King William St, & London Br.

No. 75.—**Kentish Town to London Bridge Station**—*Light Green*—*Via* Gt. College St., Pancras Rd., Gray's Inn Rd., Holborn, St Bride's St., Ludgate Hill, St Paul's, Cannon St., & London Bridge.

No. 76.—**Kentish Town to Trafalgar Square**—*Yellow*—From "Bull and Gate," *via* High Street Camden Town, Hampstead Road, Tottenham Court Road, St Martin's Lane.

No. 77.—**Kentish Town to Victoria**—*Yellow*—*Via* Lismore Road, Malden Road, Ferdinand Street, Chalk Farm Road, Charing Cross Rd., and Westminster to Victoria.

No. 78.—**Kingsland to "Elephant and Castle"**—*Dark Green*—*Via* Kingsland Road, Shoreditch, Bishopsgate Street, Gracechurch Street, London Bridge, Borough.

Trafalgar Square.

No. 79.—Kilburn to Charing Cross—*Red*—*Via* "Lord Palmerston," Maida Vale, Edgware Road, Marble Arch, Oxford Street, Regent Street, Pall Mall East.

No. 80.—Kilburn to Fulham—*Blue*—*Via* Cambridge Avenue, Walterton Road, Westbourne Park Station, Gt. Western Road, Westbourne Grove, Notting Hill Gate, Silver Street, High Street Kensington, Earl's Court Road, Redcliffe Gardens, Fulham Road.

No. 81.—Kilburn to Harlesden—*Light Green*—*Via* High Road, Palmerston Road, Christchurch Road, Willesden Lane, Craven Park, and Harrow Road.

No. 82.—Kilburn to Liverpool Street—*Dark Green*—*Via* "Lord Palmerston," Maida Vale, Edgware Rd., Marble Arch, Oxford St., Holborn, Cheapside, Bank, Moorgate St., London Wall,

No. 83.—Kilburn to Victoria Station—*Red*—*Via* Maida Vale, Edgware Road, Marble Arch, Park Lane, Piccadilly, Grosvenor Place.

No. 84.—Ladbroke Grove to London Bridge—*Red*—*Via* Ladbroke Grove, Cromwell Road, Talbot Road, Richmond Road, Westbourne Grove, Bishop's Road, Eastbourne Terrace, Praed Street, Edgware Road, Oxford Circus, Pall Mall, Charing Cross, Strand, Fleet Street, Ludgate Circus, Cannon Street, King William Street.

No. 85.—Lancaster Road to Liverpool Street—*Dark Green*—*Via* Westbourne Grove, Bishop's Road, Edgware Road, Oxford Street, Cheapside, Bank, Moorgate Street, London Wall.

No. 86.—Lee and Peckham—Rye Lane, Peckham, to "Tiger's Head," Lee Green, *via* High St. Peckham, Queen's Road, New Cross Gate, and Lewisham High Road.

No. 87.—Lee and Penge—*Via* Catford Bridge and Perry Hill.

No. 88.—Lee Green and New Cross—*Via* Lee Road and Lewisham High Road.

No. 89.—Liverpool Street to Camberwell Green—*Green*—*Via* Houndsditch, Minories, Tower Bridge, Tooley Street, Spa Road, Grange Road, and Camberwell Green.

No. 90.—Liverpool Street to Peckham Rye—*Dark Green*—*Via* Houndsditch, Minories, Tower Bridge Tooley Street, Jamaica Road, St James' Road, Ilderton Road, Canterbury Road, Loder St., St Mary's Road, Eveline Road, Nunhead Lane, and Peckham Rye.

No. 91.—Lower Sydenham—New Cross Station (S.E.R.), to Bell Green, Lower Sydenham, *via* New Cross Road, Malpas Road, Brockley, Crofton Park, Honor Oak, and Forest Hill.

No. 92.—Marylebone to Waterloo—*Via* Baker St., Regent St., Strand, Waterloo Br.

No. 93.—Merton and Tooting to Gracechurch Street—*Green*—*Via*—Lower and Upper Tooting, Balham, Clapham Common, Clapham Road, Stockwell, Kennington Park Road, "Elephant and Castle," and London Bridge.

No. 94.—Moorgate Street Station to London Bridge Station—*Chocolate, with red umbrella on top*—*Via* Moorgate Street, Princes Street, King William Street, and London Bridge.

No. 95.—New North Road and Old Kent Road—*Dark Green*—*Via* New North Road, Essex Road, City Road, Finsbury, Moorgate Street, Bank, King William Street, London Bridge, Bow, Great Dover Street, and Old Kent Road.

No. 96.—Norwood—Crystal Palace to Streatham, *via* Norwood.

No. 97.—Norwood Cemetery to Brixton Station—*Green*—*Via* Tulse Hill.

No. 98.—Nunhead—High Street Peckham, to Nunhead, *via* Rye Lane, and Peckham Rye.

No. 99.—Old Kent Road to Camden Town—*Dark Blue*—From "Dun Cow," *via* Old Kent Road "Elephant and Castle," London Road, Waterloo Bridge, Strand, Charing Cross, Regent Street, Great Portland Street, Albany Street, and Park Street.

No. 100.—Old Ford to Royal Exchange—*Yellow*—From "Marquis of Cornwallis," *via* Roman Road, Green Street, Bethnal Green Road, Bishopsgate Street, and Threadneedle Street.

No. 101.—Paddington to Charing Cross—*Red*—*Via* Bishop's Road, Eastbourne Terrace, Praed Street, Edgware Road, Oxford Street, Regent Street, and Pall Mall East.

No. 102.—Paddington to London Bridge—*Yellow*—*Via* Bishop's Road, Edgware Road, Oxford Street, Cheapside, Bank, King William Street, and London Bridge.

No. 103.—Peckham to Lordship Lane—*Green*—*Via* Rye Lane, Peckham Rye, Barry Road, and Crystal Palace Road.

No. 104.—Peckham to Old Kent Road—*Light Green*—*Via* High Street, Hill Street, Trafalgar Road to the "Lord Nelson."

No. 105.—Poplar Station to Canning Town—*Red*—*Via* East India Dock Road.

No. 106.—Portland Road Station to Charing Cross Station—*Via* Great Portland Street, New Cavendish Street, Portland Place, Regent Street, Haymarket, Pall Mall East.

No. 107.—Portobello Road to Charing Cross and London Bridge—*Red*—*Via* "Royal Oak," Praed Street, Edgware Road, Oxford Street, Regent Street, Pall Mall East, Strand, Fleet Street, Ludgate Hill, St Paul's, Cheapside, Bank, King William Street, London Bridge.

No. 108.—Putney and Brondesbury—*Orange*—*Via* Putney Sta. (L. & S.-W.), Putney High St., Putney Br., Fulham High St., Fulham Rd., North End Rd., Lillie Rd., Earl's Court Rd., Kensington High St., Church St., Silver St., Notting Hill Gate, Pembridge Villas, Richmond Rd., Great Western Rd., Walterton Rd., Cambridge Rd., High Rd., Kilburn, to Brondesbury.

No. 109.—Putney to Liverpool Street—*White*—*Via* High Street, Putney Bridge, Fulham Rd., Walham Green, Knightsbridge, Piccadilly, Charing Cross, Strand, Fleet Street, Ludgate Hill, Cheapside, Bank, Moorgate Street, London Wall.

No. 110.—Putney—"Bedford Arms." Clapham Road to "Northumberland Arms," Upper Richmond Rd., Putney, *via* Clapham High St., Clapham Common, Clapham Junction, and East Hill.

No. 111.—Putney Bridge Station to Wimbledon—*Brown*—*Via* Putney Bridge, High Street, Putney Hill, Wimbledon Common.

No 112.—Raynes Park—Clapham Junction to Raynes Park, *via* Northcote Road, Wandsworth Common Station, Trinity Road, "Wheatsheaf," Tooting, High Street Merton, and Wimbledon.

No. 113.—Richmond—Putney to Richmond, *via* Upper Richmond Road and East Sheen.

No. 114.—St George's Church (Borough) to Monument Station—*Red*—*Via* Borough High Street, London Bridge.

No. 115.—St John's Wood to Camberwell—*Light Green*—From Swiss Cottage *via* Wellington Rd., Park Rd., Baker St., Oxford St., Regent St., Charing Cross, Westminster Br., London Rd., and "Elephant and Castle."

No. 116.—St John's Wood to London Bridge Station—*Dark Green*—*Via* Oxford Street, Holborn, Cheapside, Bank, King William Street, and London Bridge.

No. 117.—St Martin's Ch. to Highgate—*Yellow*—Hampstead Rd., Camden Tn., Kentish Tn. Rd.

No. 118.—St Paul's Station to Liverpool Street Station—*Green*—*Via* Queen Victoria Street, Bank, Moorgate Street, and London Wall.

No. 119.—Shepherd's Bush to Burdett Rd.—*Light Green*—*Via* Uxbridge Rd., Notting Hill, Marble Arch, Oxford St., Holborn, Cheapside, Bank, Cornhill, Leadenhall St. Whitechapel Rd & Mile End Rd.

No. 120.—Shooters Hill—Blackheath Station (S.E.R.) to Shooters Hill Road.

No. 121.—South Hackney to Bank—*Red*—*Via* Victoria Park Road, Hackney Road, Shoreditch, Threadneedle Street.

No. 122.—Southwark Park Road to Gracechurch Street—*Dark Green*—*Via* Bermondsey, Tooley Street, and London Bridge.

No. 123.—Starch Green to Liverpool St. Sta.—*Light Green*—From "Queen of England," *via* Shepherd's Bush, Uxbridge Rd., Bayswater Rd., Oxford St., Holborn, Cheapside, Moorgate St.

No. 124.—Stoke Newington to Victoria—*Dark Green*—*Via* Abney Park Cemetery, Church St., Newington Green, Mildmay Park, Essex Rd., "Angel," St John's Street Rd., Rosebery Avenue, Gray's Inn Road, Holborn, Chancery Lane, Strand, Charing Cross, and Victoria St.

No. 125.—Stonebridge Park to Willesden—*Via* Harlesden Village and Willesden Lane.

No. 126.—Streatham to Gracechurch Street—*Green*—*Via* Streatham Hill, Brixton Road, Kennington Park Road, Borough, and London Bridge.

No. 127.—"Times"—Rye Lane, Peckham, to Oxford St., *via* Peckham Rd., Camberwell Gr., Walworth Rd., "Elephant and Castle," Westminster Br., Charing Cross, Piccadilly Circus, and Regent St.

No. 128.—Tollington Park to Victoria Station—*Dark Green*—*Via* "Stapleton Hall Tavern," Tollington Pk., Stroud Green Rd., Tollington Pk. Rd., Hornsey Rd., Seven Sisters Rd., Holloway Rd., "Angel," Pentonville Hill, Euston Rd., Gt. Portland St., Mortimer St., Regent St., Oxford Circus, New Bond St., Old Bond St., Piccadilly, Hyde Pk. Corner, Grosvenor Pl. to Victoria Station.

No. 129.—Tower Bridge—East Dulwich to Liverpool Street, *via* Peckham Rye, Rye Lane, Hill Street, Old Kent Road, Bermondsey, Dockhead, and Tower Bridge.

No. 130.—Tulse Hill to Gracechurch Street—*Green*—*Via* Brixton Road, Kennington Park Road, "Elephant and Castle," Borough, and London Bridge.

No. 131.—Turnham Green to Victoria Station—*White*—*Via* King St., Fulham Palace Rd., "Salisbury Arms," Walham Green, King's Road, Sloane Square, Buckingham Palace Road.

No. 132.—Vanbrugh Park—Blackheath Station (S.E.R.) to Charlton Road, *via* Vanbrugh Park.

No. 133.—Victoria to Holloway Road—*Yellow*—*Via* Westminster to Charing Cross, Hampstead Road, Camden Road, Parkhurst Road.

No. 134.—Victoria Station to King's Cross—*Green*—*Via* Grosvenor Pl., Piccadilly, Leicester Sq., Long Acre, Queen St., Holborn, Southampton Row, Russell Sq., Gilford St, Judd St., & Euston Rd.

No. 135.—Victoria Station to Oxford Circus—*Blue*—*Via* Grosvenor Place, Piccadilly, Bond St. and Oxford Street.

No. 136.—Walham Green and Highbury Barn—*Light Blue*—*Via* Fulham Rd., South Kensington Sta., Brompton Rd., Hyde Park Corner, Piccadilly, Shaftesbury Ave., Charing Cross Rd., Theobald's Road, Rosebery Avenue. "Angel," Islington, Upper Street, Highbury Grove.

No. 137.—Walham Green to Islington—*Dark Blue*—*Via* Fulham Road, Brompton Road, Knightsbridge, Hyde Park Corner, Park Lane, Baker Street, Marylebone Road, Euston Road, King's Cross, and Pentonville Hill to "Hare and Hounds," Upper Street.

No. 138.—Walham Green (*via* Victoria Station) **to Liverpool Street**—*White*—*Via* King's Rd., Buckingham Pal. Rd., Charing Cross, Fleet St., Cannon St., Bank, Moorgate St., London Wall.

No. 139.—Walham Green (*via* Victoria Station) **to London Bridge Station**—Same as 138 to Ludgate Hill, thence *via* Cheapside, King William Street, and London Bridge.

No. 140.—Walham Green to Shoreditch Church—*White*—*Via* Fulham Rd., Piccadilly, Fleet St., Bank, Threadneedle Street, Bishopsgate Street, and Norton Folgate.

No. 141.—Waterloo Station to Shoreditch Church—*Red*—*Via* Waterloo Bridge, Strand, Chancery Lane, Holborn, Charterhouse St., Barbican, Finsbury Sq., Worship St., and Shoreditch.

No. 142.—Wandsworth Bridge Tavern and Liverpool Street—*Brown*—*Via* Wandsworth Bridge Rd., Parson's Green. King's Rd., Sloane Sq., Lr. Sloane St., Pimlico Rd., Buckingham Pal. Rd., Victoria Sta., Victoria St., Broad Sanctuary, Parliament St., Whitehall, Charing Cross, Strand, Fleet St., Ludgate Circus, Ludgate Hill, St Paul's Church-yard, Cannon St., Queen Victoria St., Bank, Princes St., Moorgate St., Blomfield Street to Liverpool Street.

No. 143.—Waterloo Station to Liverpool Street Station—*Brown*—*Via* Stamford Street, Blackfriars Bridge, Queen Victoria Street, Moorgate Street, and London Wall.

No. 144.—Waterloo—Waterloo Station to Wellington Street, *via* Waterloo Bridge.

No. 145.—West Kensington to London Bridge Station—*Brown*—*Via* Piccadilly, Shaftesbury Avenue, Holborn, Cheapside, Bank, King William Street, and London Bridge.

No. 146.—West Kensington to Shoreditch—*Brown*—*Via* Richmond Road, Old Brompton Road, Knightsbridge, Piccadilly, Charing Cross, Strand, Fleet St., Ludgate Hill, St Paul's, Bank.

No. 147.—West Kilburn to Charing Cross—*Yellow*—*Via* Malvern Road, Shirland Road, Warwick Road, Harrow Road, Edgware Road, Marble Arch, Oxford Street, Regent St., and Pall Mall East.

No. 148.—West Kilburn to London Bridge Station—*Yellow*—Same as No. 147 to Oxford Street, thence *via* Holborn, Cheapside, Bank, King William Street, and London Bridge.

No. 149.—West Kilburn to Victoria Station—*Red*—Same as No. 147 to Marble Arch, thence *via* Park Lane, Piccadilly, and Grosvenor Place.

No. 150.—Westminster to Liverpool St. Sta.—*Brown*—From 'Monster,' *via* Lupus St., Gt. Smith St., Parliament St., Charing Cross, Fleet St., Cannon St., Bank, Moorgate St., and London Wall.

No. 151.—Westminster Bridge to Charing Cross—*Red*—*Via* Parliament Street and Whitehall.

No. 152.—Wormwood Scrubbs to London Bridge Station—*Dark Green*—*Via* St Quintin's Avenue, Cambridge Gardens, Notting Hill Station, Ladbroke Grove, Elgin Crescent, Archer Street, Westbourne Grove, Paddington, Praed Street, Edgware Road, Marble Arch, Oxford Street, Holborn, Newgate Street, Cheapside, Bank, King William Street, over London Bridge.

PRINCIPAL LONDON CLUBS.

Plate No.

Club	Plate	No.
Albemarle, 13 Albemarle Street ..	Bb	7
Alexandra (Ladies), 12 Grosvenor St., W.	Ab	7
Alliance (Ladies'), 37 Clarges St., W.	Ac	7
Alpine, 23 Savile Row, W.	Bb	7
American Society in London, 114 Southampton Row, W.C. ..	Cc	8
Army and Navy, 36 Pall Mall ..	Bc	7
Arthur's, 69 St James's Street ..	Bc	7
Arts, 40 Dover Street, W.	Bb	7
Arundel, 1 Adelphi Terrace, W.C. ..	Cb	7
Athenæum, 107 Pall Mall ..	Bb	7
Authors', 3 Whitehall Court ..	Cc	7
Automobile, 119 Piccadilly ..	Ac	7
Bachelors', 8 Hamilton Place, W. ..	Ac	7
Badminton, 100 Piccadilly, W. ..	Ac	7
Baldwin, 79a Pall Mall	Bc	7
Bath (Ladies' & Gent.), 16 Berkeley St.	Bb	7
Beaufort, 34 Soho Square	Bc	8
Boodle's, 28 St James's Street ..	Bb	7
Brooks's, 59 St James's Street ..	Bb	7
Burlington Fine Arts, 17 Savile Row ..	Bb	7
Caledonian, 30 Charles Street, S.W...	Bb	7
Camera, 28 Charing Cross Road ..	Cb	7
Capital & Counties, 42 Bow Lane, E.C.	Bc	6
Carlton, 94 Pall Mall	Bc	7
Cavalry, 127 Piccadilly	Ac	7
City Athenæum, Angel Court, E.C.	Bb	6
City Carlton, 24 St Swithin's Lane ..	Bc	6
City Liberal, Walbrook	Bc	6
City of London, 19 Old Broad St., E.C.	Cb	6
City of London Chess, 7 Grocers' Hall Court, Poultry	Bc	6
Cocoa Tree, 64 St James's Street ..	Bc	7
Colonial, 4 Whitehall Court ..	Cc	7
Conservative, 74 St James's Street ..	Bc	7
Constitutional, Northumberland Av.	Cb	7
Crichton, 39 King Street, W.C. ..	Cb	7
Denison (Ladies) 15 Buckingham St., Strand	Cb	7
Devonshire, 50 St James's Street ..	Bb	7
E. India United Ser., 16 St James's Sq.	Bb	7
Eccentric, 21 Shaftesbury Avenue ..	Bb	7
Eighty, 3 Hare Court, Temple	Db	7
Eldon, 27 Chancery Lane	Dc	8
Empire (Ladies'), 4 Whitehall Court ..	Cc	7
Empress (Ladies'), 35 Dover Street ..	Bb	7
Farmers', Salisbury Square Hotel ..	Eb	7
Foreign Missions, 149 Highbury New Pk.	Bb	9
Garrick, 15 Garrick St., Covent Garden	Cb	7
German Athenæum, 93 Mortimer St., W.	Bc	8
Golfers', 2A Whitehall Court	Cc	7
Grafton, 10 Grafton Street, W. ..	Bb	7
Green Park (Ladies'), 10 Grafton Street	Bb	7
Green Room, 20 Bedford Street, W.C.	Cb	7
Gresham, 1 Gresham Place, E.C. ..	Bc	6
Grosvenor, 135 New Bond Street, W.	Ab	7
Grosvenor Cres. (Ladies), 15 Grosvenor Cr.	Ab	7
Guards', 70 Pall Mall	Bc	7
Gun Club, 4 Carlton Street, S.W. ..	Bb	7
Hogarth, 175 New Bond Street, W. ..	Bb	7
Hurlingham, Fulham	Bc	12
Hyde Park, 128 Piccadilly	Ac	7
Imperial Colonies, 53 Victoria Street	Bd	7
Imperial Service, 84 Piccadilly ..	Ac	7
Isthmian, 105 Piccadilly	Ac	7
Junior Army & Navy, 10 St James's St.	Bc	7
Junior Athenæum, 116 Piccadilly ..	Ac	7
Junior Carlton, 30 to 35 Pall Mall ..	Bb	7
Junior Conservative, 43 Albemarle St.	Bb	7
Junior Constitutional, 101 Piccadilly	Ac	7
Junior Naval and Military, 97 Piccadilly	Ac	7
Junior United Service, 11 Charles St., St James's	Bb	7
Kennel, 7 Grafton St., New Bond, St.	Bb	7
Ladies' Chess, 31 Dover St., Piccadilly	Bb	7
Ladies' County, 21 Hanover Square ..	Ba	7
Law Society, 103 Chancery Lane ..	Dc	8
Lord's (M.C.C.), St John's Wood Rd.	Ca	11
Marlborough. 52 Pall Mall, S.W... ..	Bc	7
National, 1 Whitehall Gardens ..	Cc	7
National Liberal, Whitehall Place, S.W.	Cc	7
National Sporting, 43 King Street, Covent Garden	Cb	7
Naval and Military, 94 Piccadilly ..	Ac	7
New Club, 4 Grafton Street	Bb	7
New County (Ladies), 21 Hanover Sq.	Ab	7
New Lyric, Princes Buildings, Coventry Street, W.	Cb	7
New Oxford and Cam., 68 Pall Mall ..	Bc	7
New Reform, St Ermin's Hotel, Westm.	Bd	7
New University, 57 St James's Street	Bb	7
New Victorian, 30a Sackville Street	Bb	7
Nimrod, 12 St James's Square ..	Bb	7
Oriental, 18 Hanover Square, W. ..	Aa	7
Orleans, 29 King Street, St James's ..	Bb	7
Oxford and Cambridge, 71-76 Pall Mall	Bc	7
Palace, 9 Bridge Street	Cc	7
Piccadilly, 128 Piccadilly	Ac	7
Pioneers' (Ladies), 5 Grafton Street	Bb	7
Portland, 9 St James's Square	Bb	7
Press, 7 Wine Office Court	Ea	7
Primrose, 5 Park Place, St James's ..	Bc	7
Prince's Racquet, Knightsbridge ..	Dc	11
Queen's, Palliser Road, W. Kensington	Ba	12
Raleigh, 16 Regent Street, S.W. ..	Bb	7
Ranelagh, Barn Elms	Ca	17
Reform, 104 Pall Mall, S.W.	Bc	7
Royal Colonial Inst., Northumberland Av.	Cb	7
Royal London Yacht, 2 Savile Row ..	Bb	7
Royal Societies', 63 St James's Street	Bc	7
Royal Thames Yacht, 7 Albemarle St.	Bb	7
Royal Water Colour, 5a Pall Mall, E.	Cb	7
St George's, 4 Hanover Square, W.	Ba	7
St George's Chess, 87 St James's Street	Bc	7
St James's, 106 Piccadilly	Ac	7
St Stephen's, 1 Bridge Street, Westm.	Cc	7
Sandringham (Ladies), 38 Dover Street	Bb	7
Savage, 6 Adelphi Terrace	Cb	7
Savile, 107 Piccadilly, W.	Ac	7
Sesame (Ladies'), 28 Dover Street ..	Bb	7
Smithfield Cattle, 12 Hanover Square	Ba	7
Sports, 8 St James's Square	Bb	7
Thatched House, 86 St James's Street	Bc	7
Travellers', 106 Pall Mall	Bb	7
Turf, 47 Clarges Street, Piccadilly ..	Ac	7
Union, Trafalgar Square	Cb	7
United Service, 116 Pall Mall ..	Cb	7
United University, 1 Suffolk Street	Cb	7
University for Ladies, 4 George St., W.	Bb	7
Victoria, 18 Wellington Street, W.C.	Db	7
Wellington, 1 Grosvenor Place	Ac	7
Whitehall, 47 Parliament Street ..	Cc	7
White's, 37 St James's Street ..	Bb	7
Windham, 13 St James's Square ..	Bb	7
Writers' (Ladies), Norfolk St., Strand	Db	7
Yorick, 30 Bedford Street, Strand ..	Cb	7

Two
ATLAS AND STREET GUIDE
OF LONDON 1908

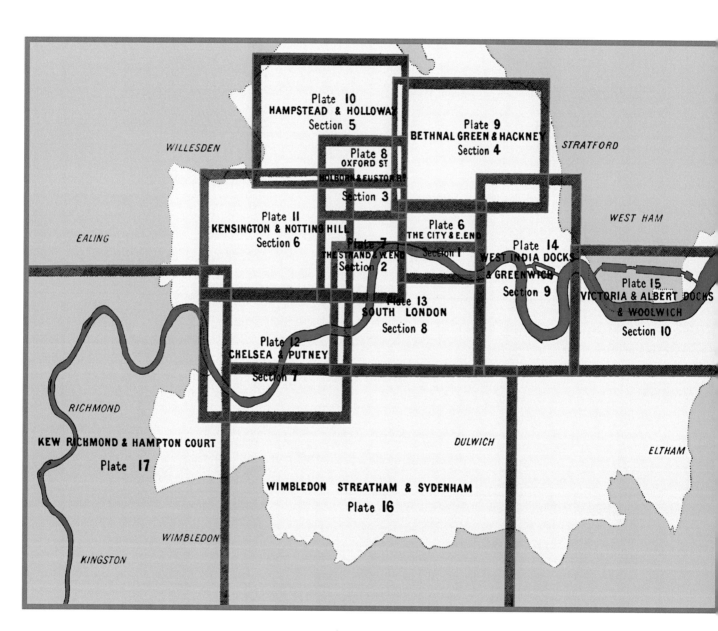

Index to Section Maps.

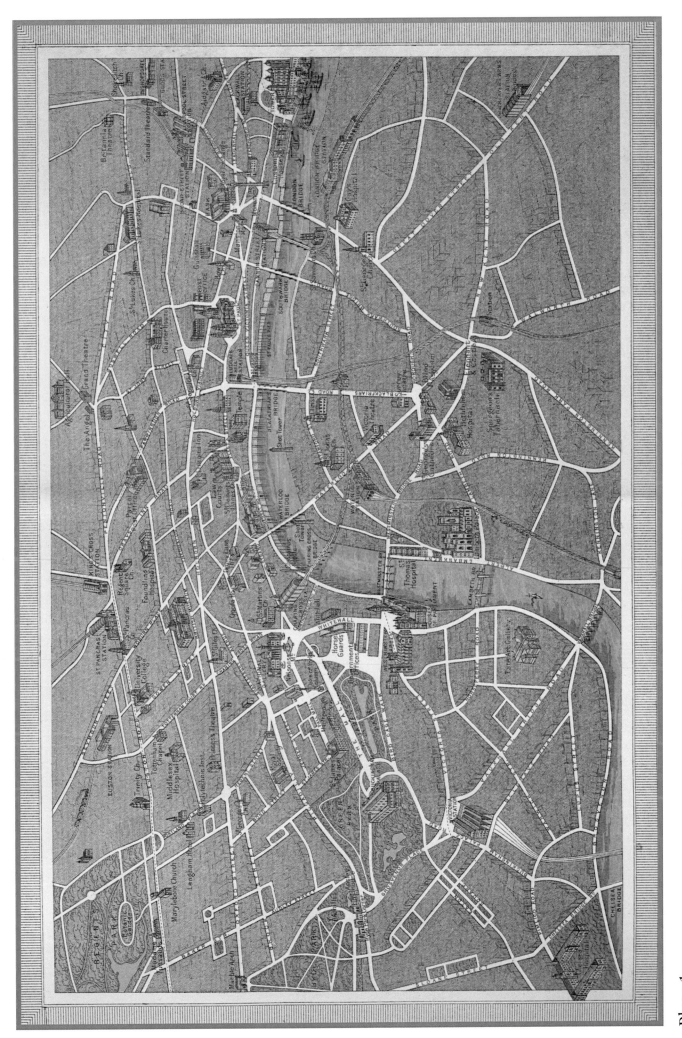

Birds Eye View Map of Central London.

Plate 1.

49

Plate 2.

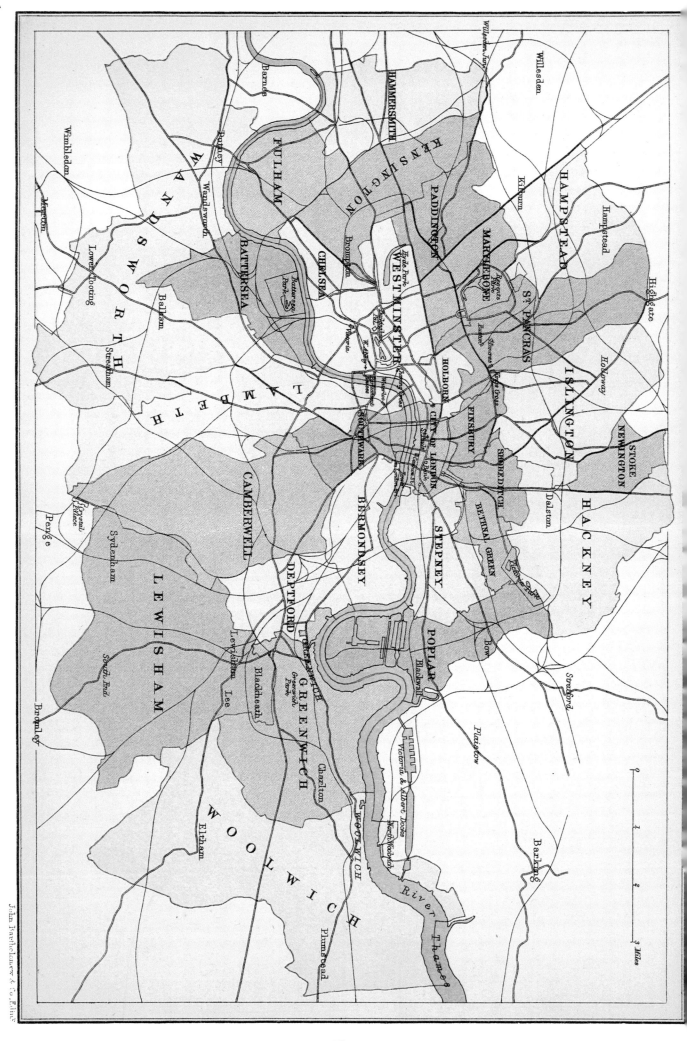

London Metropolitan Boroughs.

John Bartholomew & Co. Edin

Plate 3.

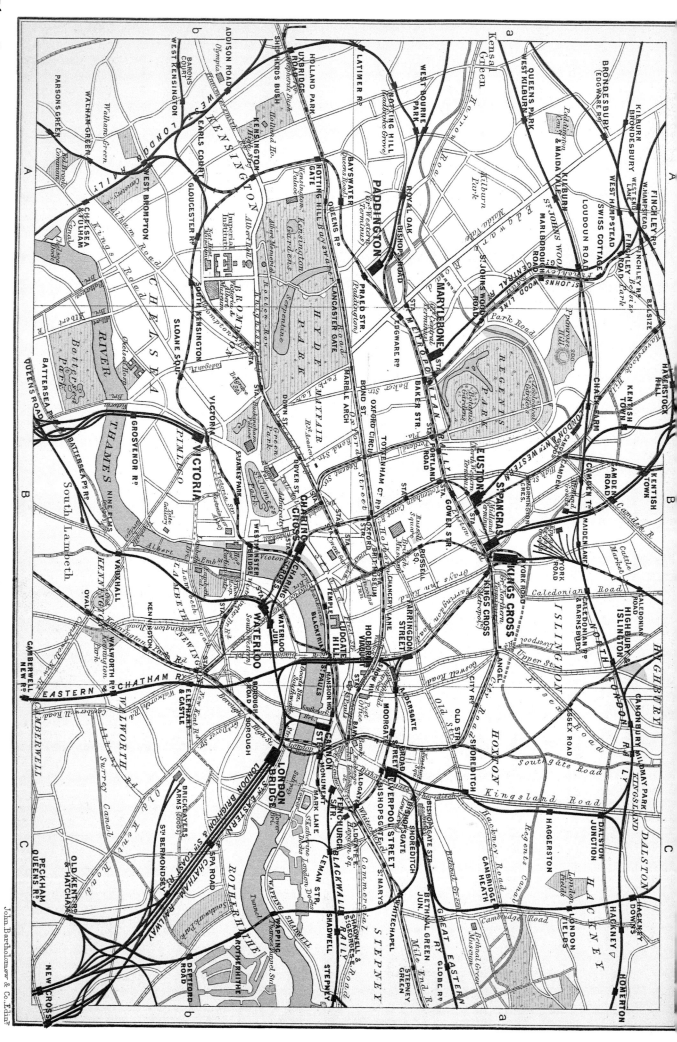

Railway Map of Central London.

John Bartholomew & Co. Edin.

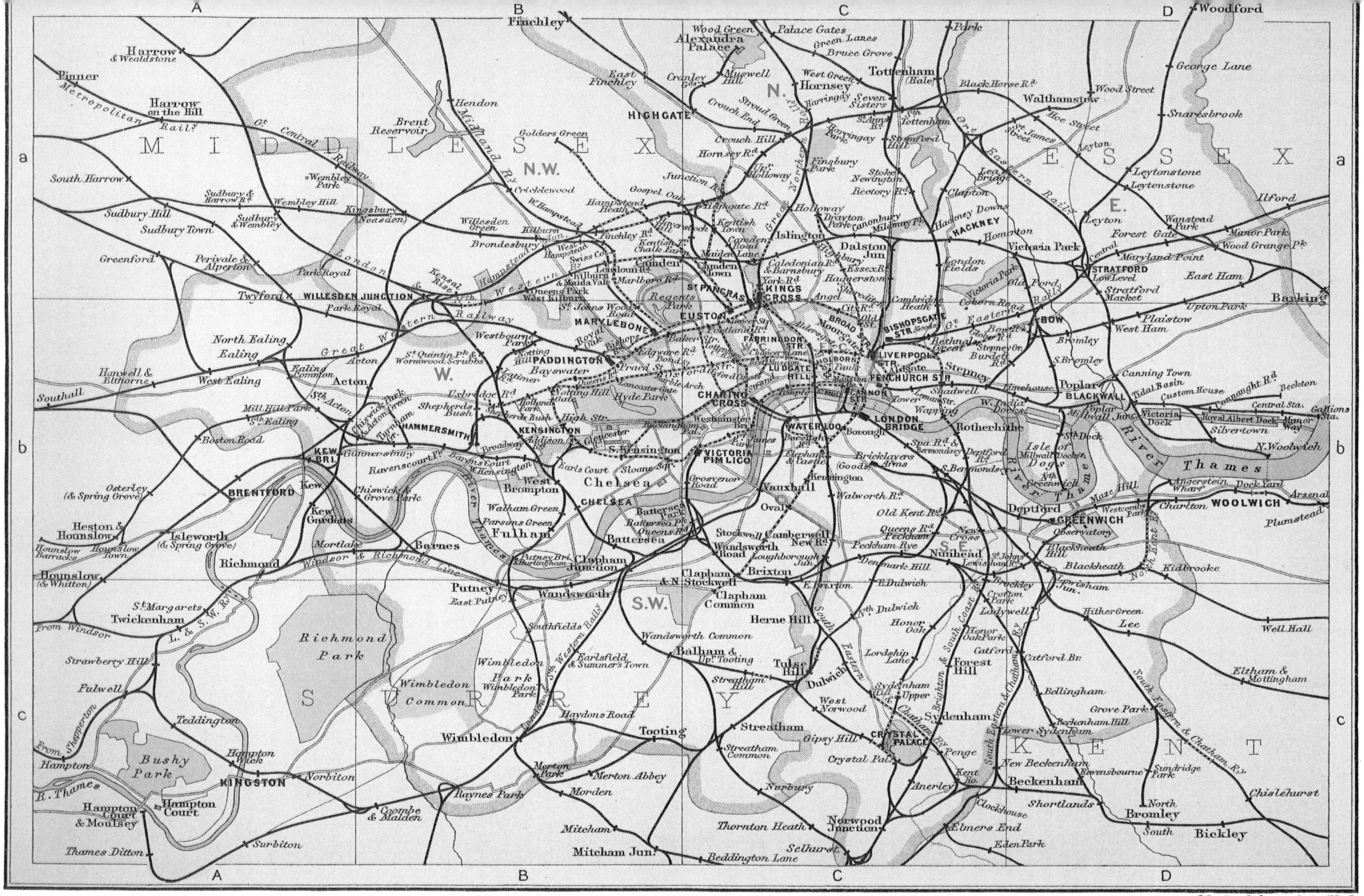

Plate 4.

London and Suburbs, Railways and Postal Districts.

John Bartholomew & Co. Edinr

54

Plate 5.

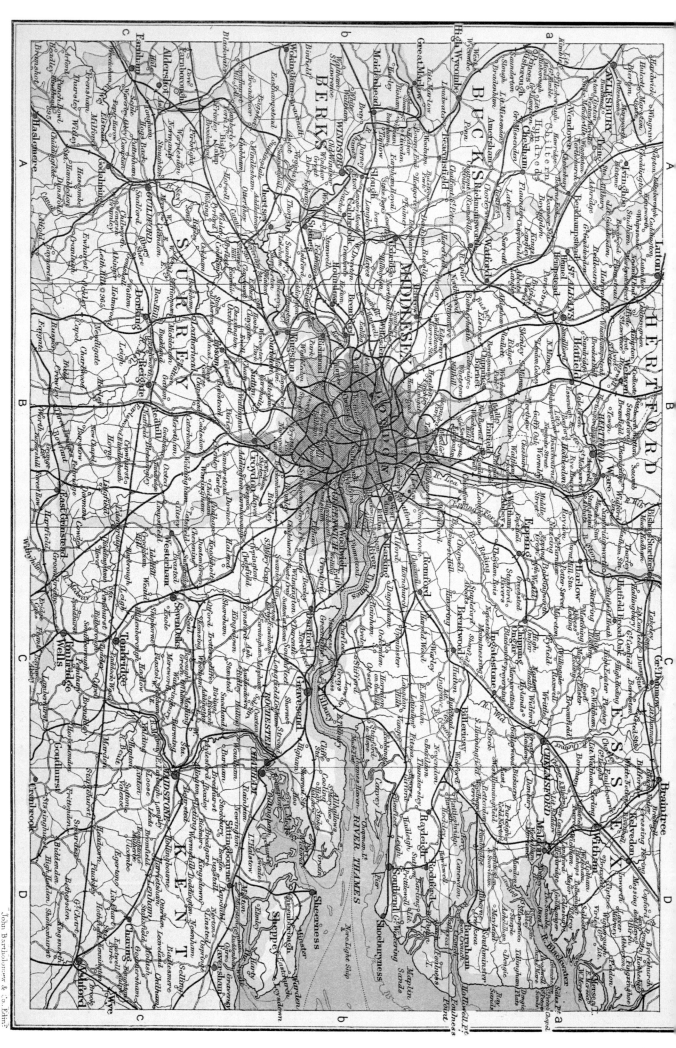

Railway Map of Environs of London.

John Bartholomew & Co. Edin?

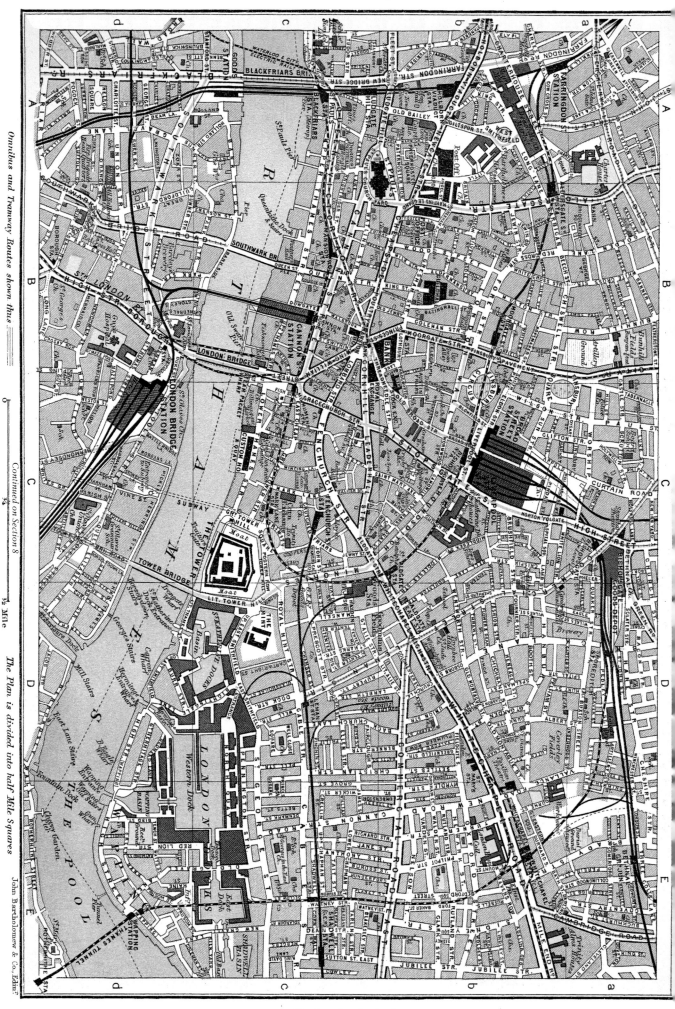

Plate 6.

STREET PLAN, SECTION 1 - THE CITY AND EAST END

Omnibus and Tramway Routes shown thus

Continued on Section 8

The Plan is divided into half Mile Squares

John Bartholomew & Co., Edin!

Continued on Sections 6 & 7

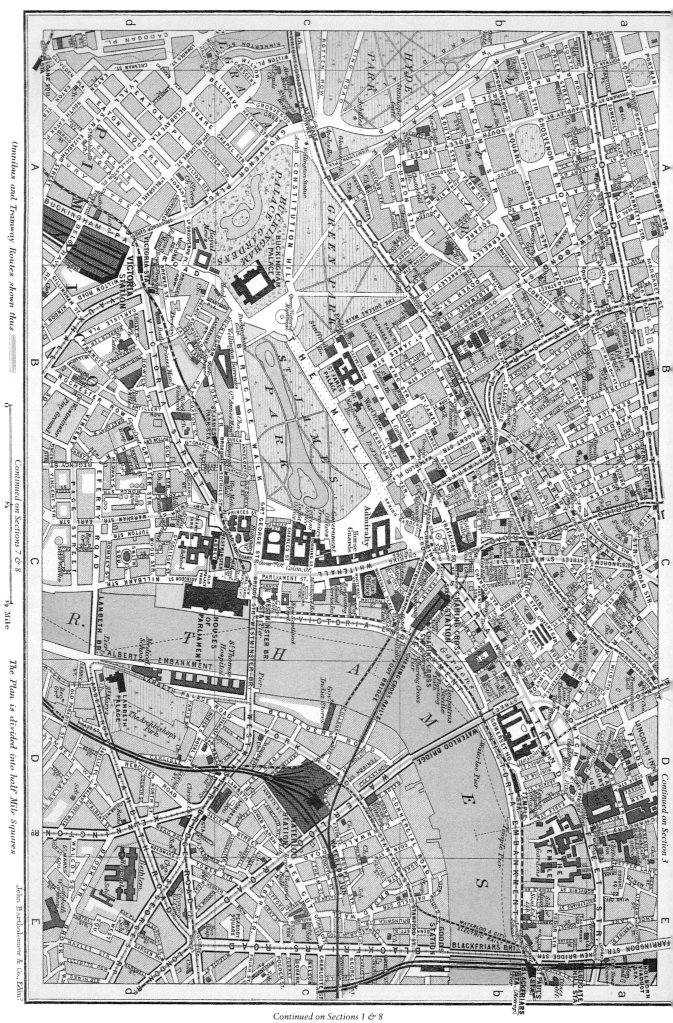

Plate 7.

STREET PLAN, SECTION 2 - THE STRAND AND WEST END

Omnibus and Tramway Routes shown thus

STREET PLAN

Continued on Sections 7 & 8

The Plan is divided into half Mile Squares

½ Mile

John Bartholomew & Co., Edin.ʳ

Continued on Section 3

Continued on Sections 1 & 8

General Index to Streets and Railway Stations.

	Plate No.		Plate No.		Plate No.

Downs Park-rd., Hackney Cb 9
Drayton-gar., Old Bromp. Ca 12
  ,,   pk. and sta. .. Ab 9
Drew-rd., Silvertown .. Ca 15
Driffield-rd., Roman-rd. Dc 9
Drummond-cres.,Easton-sq.Ca8
  ,,   rd.,B'rm'nds'y Db13
  ,,   st., Easton-sq. Bb 8
Drury-lane .. .. .. Cc 8
Duckett-st., Stepney .. Bb 14
Dudding Hill Station .. Ba 4
Dufferin-st., Bunhill-row Ba 6
Duke-st., Aldgate-st. .. Cb 6
  ,,   st., Manchester-sq. Db 11
  ,,   st., St James' .. Bb 7
  ,,   st., Stamford-st. Eb 7
  ,,   st., Villier's-st. Cb 7
Dulwich Station .. .. Cc 4
Duncan-ter., City-rd. .. Ac 9
Duncannon-st., Strand .. Cb 7
Dundee Wharf, Wapping Ed 6
Dundonald-st., Westm. ..Ab 13
Dunk-st., Spitalfields .. Db 6
Dunlace-rd., Homerton Db 9
Dunloe-st., Hackney-rd. Cc 9
Dunsany-rd., W. Kens. Ad 11
Dunston-st., Kingsland-rd. Cc 9
Durham-rd., Seven Sisters
          road Da 10
Durham-st., Strand .. Cb 7
  ,,   ter., Westbo.-pk. Bb11
  ,,   vills., Kensingt'n Bc 11
Durrington-rd., Homerton Db 9
Dyott-st., New Oxford-st. Cc 8
Eagle-st., Holborn .. Dc 8
Eagle Wharf-rd., Hoxton Bc 9
Ealing Common station .. Ab 4
Ealing Station .. .. Ab 4
Eardley-cr., W. Br'mpton Ba 12
Earl-st., Borough Bb13
  ,,   st., Finsbury .. Cb 6
  ,,   st., Lisson-gro. ..Cb 11
  ,,   st., Millbank.. .. Cd 7
  ,,   st., Seven Dials .. Ca 7
Earl's Court .. .. Ba 12
  ,,   rd., Kens'gton Ba 12
  ,,   sq. .. .. Ba 12
  ,,   station .. Ab 3
Earlsfield station .. .. Bc 4
Eastbourne-ter., Padd'gt'nCb11
Eastcheap .. .. .. Cc 6
Easton-st., Exmouth-st. Db 8
Eastwood-rd., Vict. Dock Ba 15
East-rd., City-rd. .. .. Bd 9
  ,,   st., Greenwich ..De 14
  ,,   st., Manchester-sq. Ac 8
  ,,   st., Red Lion-sq. .. Db 8
  ,,   st., Walworth-rd. ..Cb 13
  ,,   st., Woolwich .. Bb 15
  ,,   Arbour-st Stepney Bb 14
  ,,   Brixton station .. Cc 4
  ,,   Dulwich station .. Cc 4
  ,,   Ferry-rd., Millwall Cd 14
  ,,   Finchley station .. Ba 4
  ,,   Ham Station .. Da 4
  ,,   India Dock-rd. ..Cc 14
  ,,   India Dock Wall-rd. Dc 14
  ,,   Putney station .. Bc 4
  ,,   Sheen .. Bb 17
  ,,   Smithfield,Lon.Docks Dc6
  ,,   Surrey-gro. .. Cc 13
Eaton-pl. & sq., Pimlico Ad 7
Eaton-ter., Pimlico ..Da 12
Ebury-st., Pimlico .. Ad 7
Eccles-rd., Lavender-hill Dc 12
Eccleston-sq., Belgrave-rd.Da12

Eccleston-st., Pimlico .. Ad 7
Edbrook-rd.,St Peter's-pk. Bb11
Eden-gr., Holloway ··Db 10
Edgware-rd. .. .. Cb 11
  ,,   station .. .. Ba 3
Edinburgh-rd., N. Kens. Ab 11
Edith-gr., W. Brompton Cb 12
Edith-rd., W. Kensington Ba12
Edmund-pl., Jewin-st. .. Bb 6
Edward-st., Deptford .. Be 14
  ,,   st., Hampst'd-rd. Ba 8
  ,,   st., City-rd. .. Bc 9
  ,,   st., Bethnal-gr. Cd 9
Edwardes-sq., Kensington Bd11
Eel Pie Island Ab17
Egerton-cres., Brompton Ca 12
  ,,   gars., Brompton Ca 12
Eglinton-rd,, Old Ford .. Dc 9
  ,,   rd., Woolwich Dc 15
Eland-rd., Lavender-hill Dc 12
  ,,   rd., Woolwich ..Cb 15
Elderfield-rd., Clapton .. Db 9
Eldon-rd., Kensington ..Cd 11
Eldon-st., Liverpool-st... Cb 6
Eleanor-rd., Hackney .. Cb 9
Elephant & Castle .. Bb 13
  ,,   station Cb 3
Elgin-av., Harrow-rd. .. Bb11
  ,,   cres.,Ladbroke-gro. Bb11
  ,,   ter., Maida-hill .. Ac10
Elizabeth-rd.,N.Woolwich Ca15
Ellen-st., Comercial-rd. Dc 6
Ellerdale-rd., Hampstead Ab10
Ellesmere-rd., Old Ford Dc 9
Elmers End station .. Cc 4
Elmore-st., Islington .. Bc 9
Elm-st., Plumstead ..Db15
  ,,   Park-gar., Chelsea Ca 12
  ,,   Park-rd., Chelsea ..Ca 12
  ,,   Tree-rd,,StJohn's-wd. Ac10
Elsa-st., Stepney Bb14
Elsdale-st., Hackney .. Dc 9
Elsley-rd., Clapham .. Dc 12
Elsham-rd., W. Kensing. Ac 11
Elsted-st., Walworth ..Cb 13
Elsworthy-rd., Primrose-hl.Bc10
Eltham station .. .. Dc 4
Elvaston-pl., S. Kens. ..Cd11
Elwood-st., Highbury-vale Aa 9
Ely-pl., Charterhouse-st. Ec 8
Embankment-sta. .. Bb 3
Emerson-st., Southwark Bc 6
Emmett-st., Poplar .. Cc 14
Emperor's-gate .. .. Ca 12
Empson-st., Bromley .. Cb 14
Endell-st., Long Acre .. Cc 8
Endsleigh-gar., Euston-sq. Cb8
  ,,   st., Euston-sq. Cb 8
England's-la., Haverstock
          hill Bb 10
Englefield-rd.,Kingsl'd-rd. Bb 9
Ennismore-gds., Knights-
          bridge Cc 11
Erasmus-st., Westminster Ab13
Ernest-st., Mile End .. Bb14
Errol-st., Bunhill-row .. Ba 6
Essex-rd. and sta., Isl'gt'n Ac 9
  ,,   st., Strand .. Db 7
  ,,   villas., Kensington Bc 11
Estcourt-rd., Fulham .. Bb 12
Este-rd., Clapham J'ction Cc 12
Ethelburga-st., Battersea Cb 12
Etheldred-st., Lambeth Bb 13
Eton-av., Hampstead ..Ab 10
  ,,   rd., Haverstock-hill Bb 10
  ,,   rd., Woolwich ..Db 15

Eugenia-rd., Oldfield-rd. Bd 14
Euston-rd. .. .. .. Bb 8
  ,,   sq., Euston-rd. .. Cb 8
  ,,   station .. .. Ba 3
  ,,   st., Euston-sq. .. Bb 8
Evelyn-gds., S. K'nsingt'n Ca12
  ,,   rd., Vict. Dock .. Ba 15
  ,,   st., Deptford .. Bd 14
Evering-rd., Stoke Newn. Ca 9
Everington-rd., Fulham Aa 12
Everlett-st., Nine Elms .. Ac 13
Eversholt-st., Camden-tn. Ba 8
Eversleigh-rd., Clapham Dc 12
Ewer-st., Southwark .. Ad 6
Exeter-st., Strand .. Db 7
Exhibition-rd., S. Kens. Cd 11
Exmouth-st., Clerkenwell Eb 8
  ,,   st., Euston-sq. Bb 8
  ,,   st., Stepney .. Bb 14
Exton-st., Waterloo-rd. Dc 7
Eyre-st. Hill, Clerkenwell Db 8
Fairbridge-rd., Holloway Ca 10
Fairfax-rd., Finchley-rd. Ab 10
Fairfield-rd., Bow-rd. .. Ec 9
Fairfoot-rd., Bow .. ..Cb 14
Fairhazel-gar., Hampst'd Ab 10
Fairholme-rd., W. Kens. Ba 12
Falcon-rd., Clapham Jun. Cc 12
Falcon-sq., Aldersgate .. Bb 6
Falkland-rd., Kentish-tn. Cb 10
Falmouth-rd.,NewK'nt-rd. Cb13
Fann-st., Aldersgate-st. Ba 6
Fanshaw-st., Hoxton .. Bc 9
Faraday-rd., Westbn.-pk. Bb 11
  ,,   st., Walworth ..Cb 13
Farleigh-rd., Stoke-Newn. Cb 9
Farm-la., Walham Green Bb 12
  ,,   st., Mayfair.. .. Ab 7
Farmer's-rd., Kenn.-pk. Bc 13
Faroe-rd., Brook-green Ad 11
Farrance-st., Limehouse Cc 14
Farringdon-av. .. .. Ec 8
  ,,   rd. .. .. Eb 8
  ,,   st. .. .. Ab 6
  ,,   st. station .. Ba 3
Fashion-st., Spitalfields .. Db 6
Favart-rd., Fulham .. Bb 12
Fawcett-rd., Rotherhithe
          New-rd. Bd 14
Fawe Pk.-rd., Putney .. Bc 12
Featherstone-st.,Bunhl.-fds. Ba6
Felden-st., Fulham .. Bb 12
Felix-st., Westm. Br.-rd. Dc 7
Fellbrigg-st., Cambr.-rd. Ea 6
Fellows-rd., Adelaide-rd. Bb 10
Felton-st., Hoxton .. Bc 9
Fenchurch-avenue .. Cc 6
  ,,   st. .. .. Cc 6
  ,,   st. station .. Cb 3
Fenelon-rd., Earl's-co. .. Ba 12
Fentiman-rd., Lambeth.. Ac 13
Fenwick-st., Woolwich .. Cc 15
Ferdinand-st., Chalk-Farm
          road Bb 10
Fermoy-av., Harrow-rd. Bb 11
Ferncroft-av., Hampstead Aa 10
Fernshaw-rd., Fulham-rd. Cb 12
Ferntower-rd., Highbury Bb 9
Fetter-la., Fleet-st. .. Ec 8
Field-rd., H'smith .. Aa 12
Fieldgate-st., Whitechapel Db6
Finborough-rd., W. Brom. Ba12
Finch-la., Cornhill .. Cc 6
Finchley-rd., St J'hn's-wd. Ab10
  ,,   rd. station .. Cb 3
Finsbury-circus .. .. Cb 6

61

Plate 8.

STREET PLAN, SECTION 3 - OXFORD STREET, HOLBORN AND EUSTON ROAD

Omnibus and Tramway Routes shown thus

The Plan is divided into half Mile Squares

John Bartholomew & Co., Edinʳ

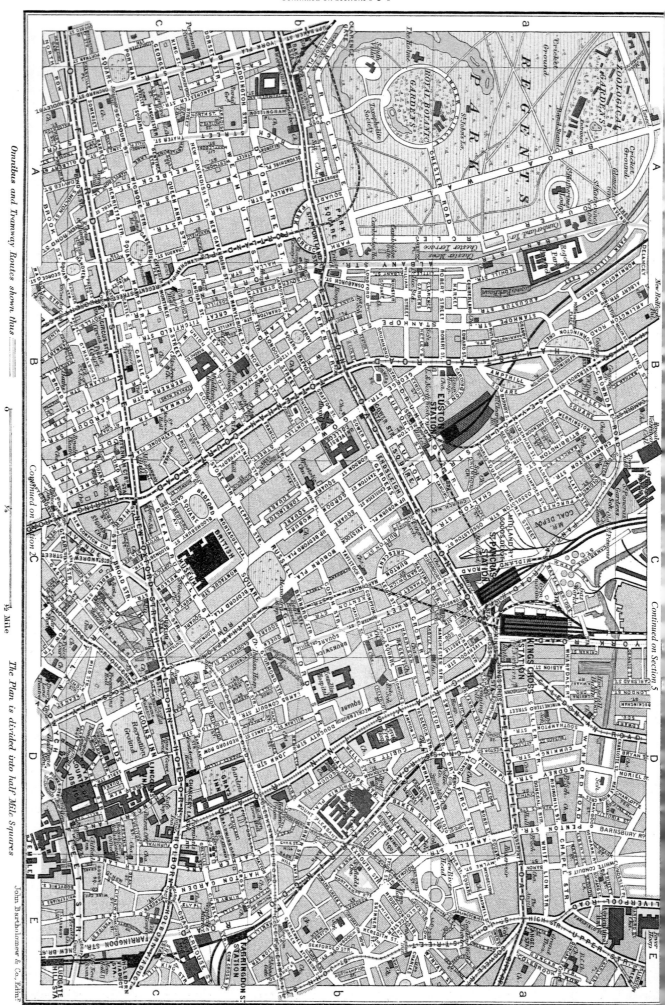

Plate 9.

STREET PLAN, SECTION 4 - BETHNAL GREEN AND HACKNEY

Omnibus and Tramway Routes shown thus

Continued on Sections 1 & 9

0   ¼   ½   ¾   1 Mile

The Plan is divided into Mile Squares

John Bartholomew & Co., Edin.ʳ

Continued on Sections 1 & 4

Plate 10.

STREET PLAN, SECTION 5 - HAMPSTEAD AND HOLLOWAY

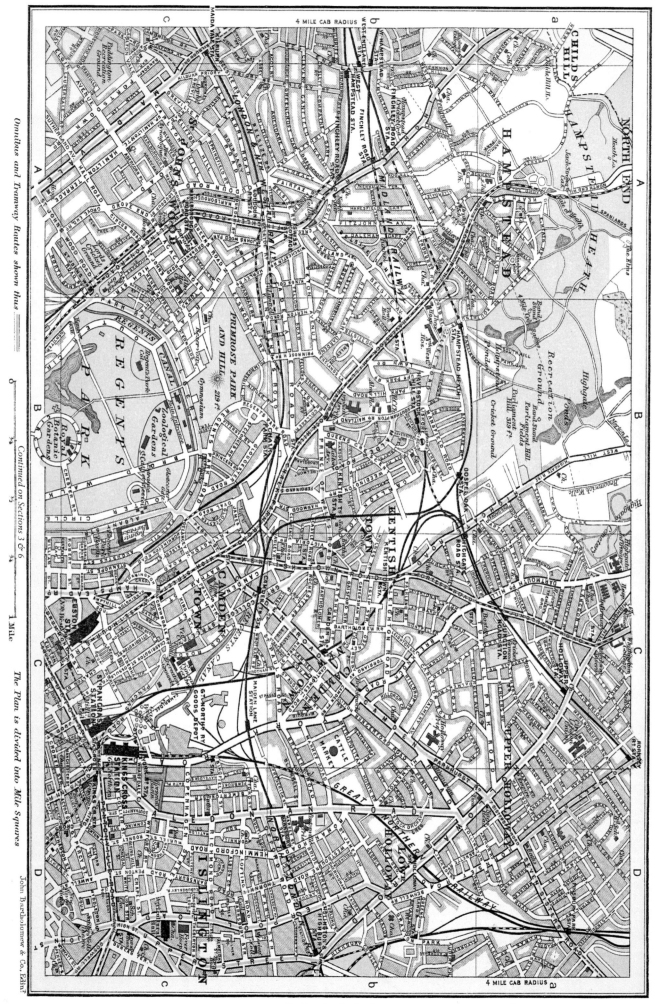

Omnibus and Tramway Routes shown thus

Continued on Sections 3 & 6

The Plan is divided into Mile Squares

John Bartholomew & Co. Edinʳ

4 MILE CAB RADIUS

Continued on Section 4

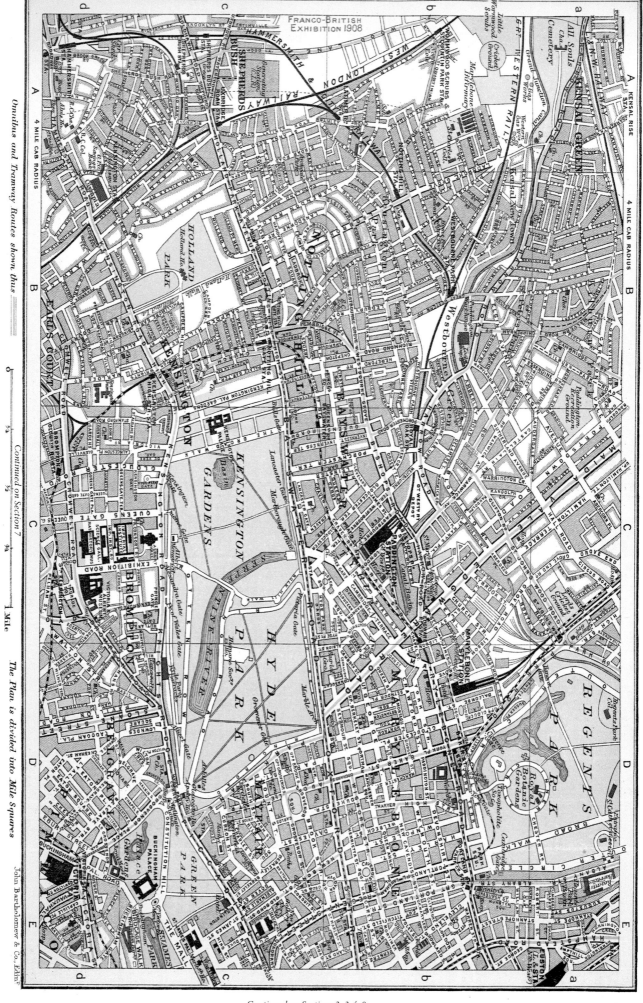

Plate 11.

STREET PLAN, SECTION 6 - KENSINGTON AND NOTTING HILL

Omnibus and Tramway Routes shown thus

Continued on Section 7

0   ¼   ½   ¾   1 Mile

The Plan is divided into Mile Squares

John Bartholomew & Co., Edin.ʳ

FRANCO-BRITISH
EXHIBITION 1908

Continued on Sections 2, 3 & 8

Plate 12.

STREET PLAN, SECTION 7 - CHELSEA AND PUTNEY

Omnibus and Tramway Routes shown thus ====

Scale of One Mile

0   ¼   ½   ¾   1 Mile

The Plan is divided into Mile Squares

John Bartholomew & Co. Edin

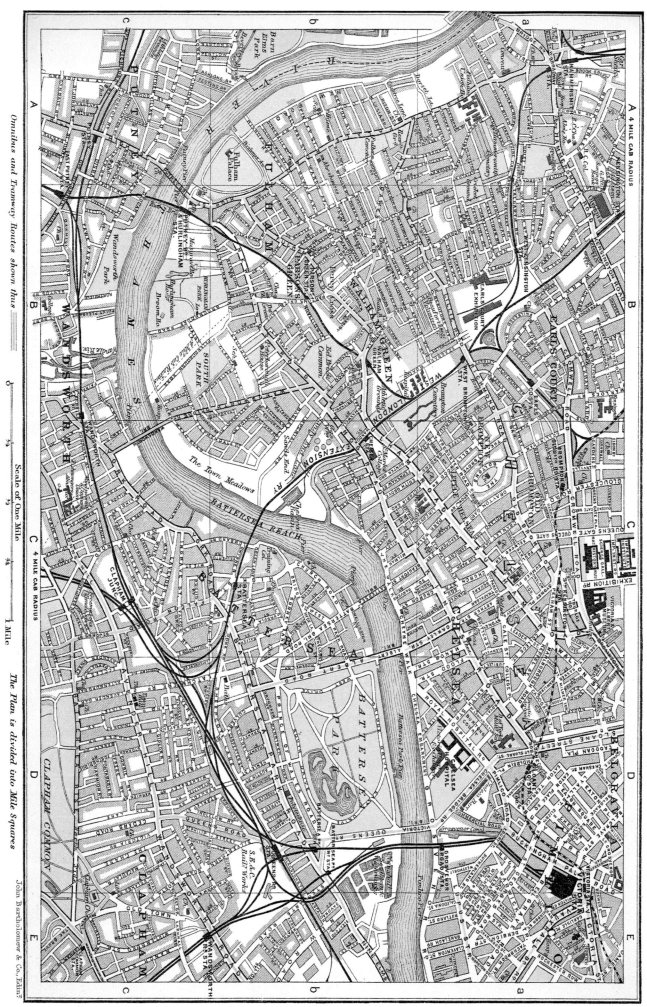

A 4 MILE CAB RADIUS

C 4 MILE CAB RADIUS

Continued on Sections 2 & 8

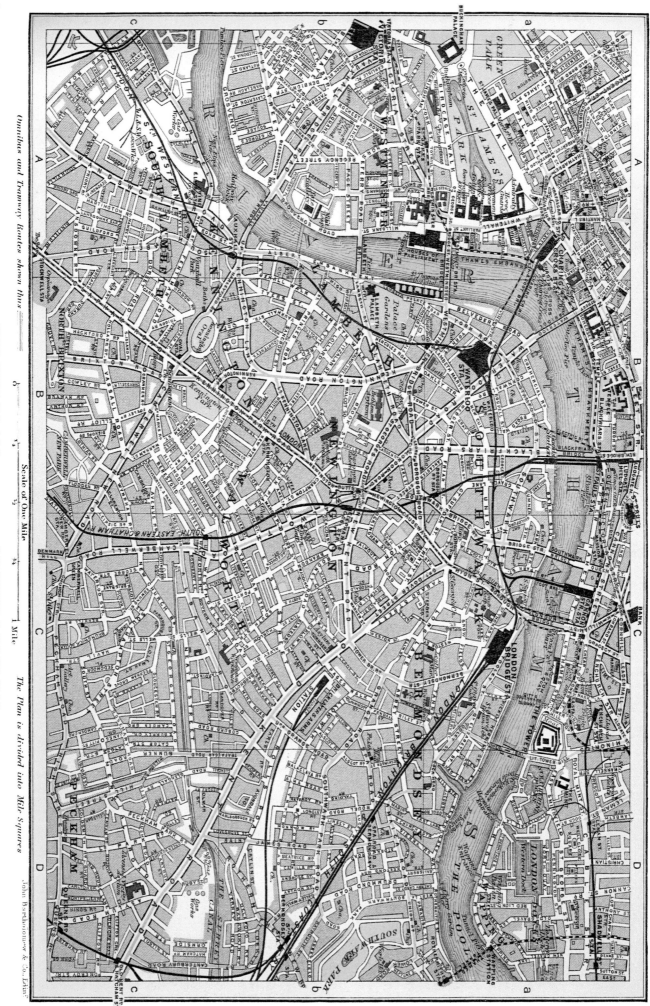

Plate 13.

STREET PLAN, SECTION 8 - SOUTH LONDON

Omnibus and Tramway Routes shown thus

Scale of One Mile

The Plan is divided into Mile Squares

John Bartholomew & Co. Edin.

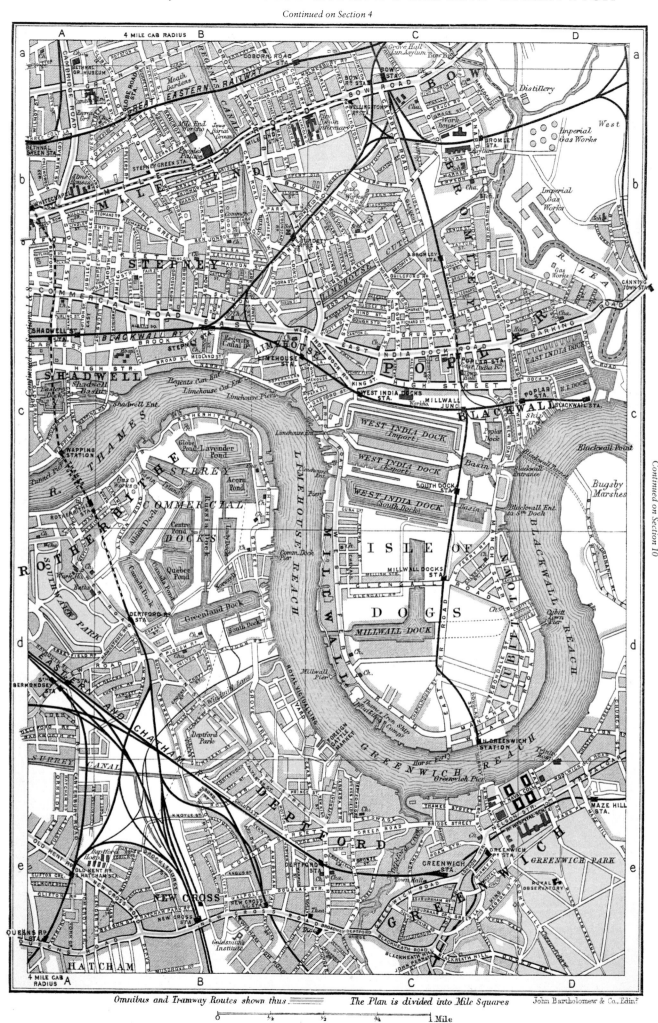

Omnibus and Tramway Routes shown thus ═══   The Plan is divided into Mile Squares   John Bartholomew & Co., Edin.

0   ¼   ½   ¾   1 Mile

74

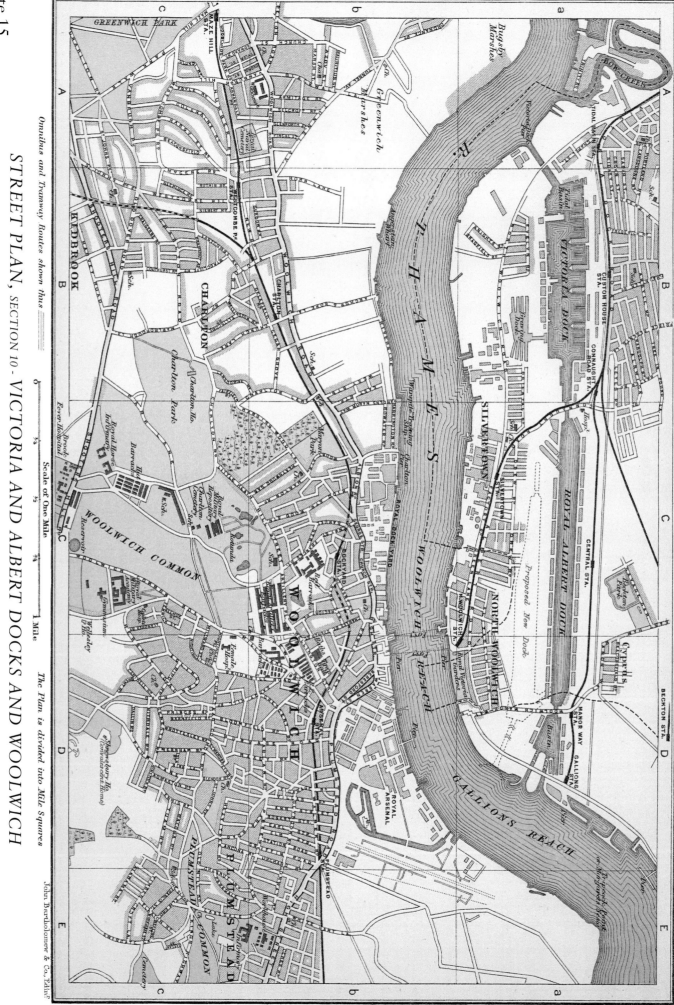

Plate 15.

STREET PLAN, SECTION 10 - VICTORIA AND ALBERT DOCKS AND WOOLWICH

Omnibus and Tramway Routes shown thus

Scale of One Mile

The Plan is divided into Mile Squares

John Bartholomew & Co., Edin.ʳ

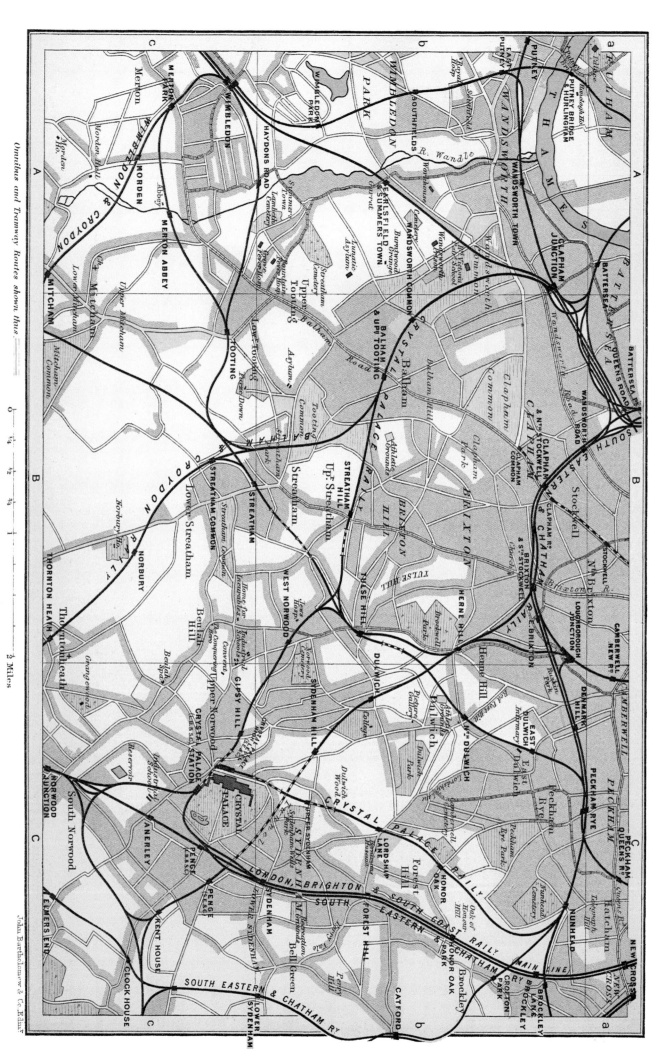

Plate 16.

WIMBLEDON, STREATHAM AND SYDENHAM

Omnibus and Tramway Routes shown thus

0   ¼   ½   ¾   1   2 Miles

John Bartholomew & Co. Edin.ʳ

Plate 17.

KEW, RICHMOND AND HAMPTON COURT

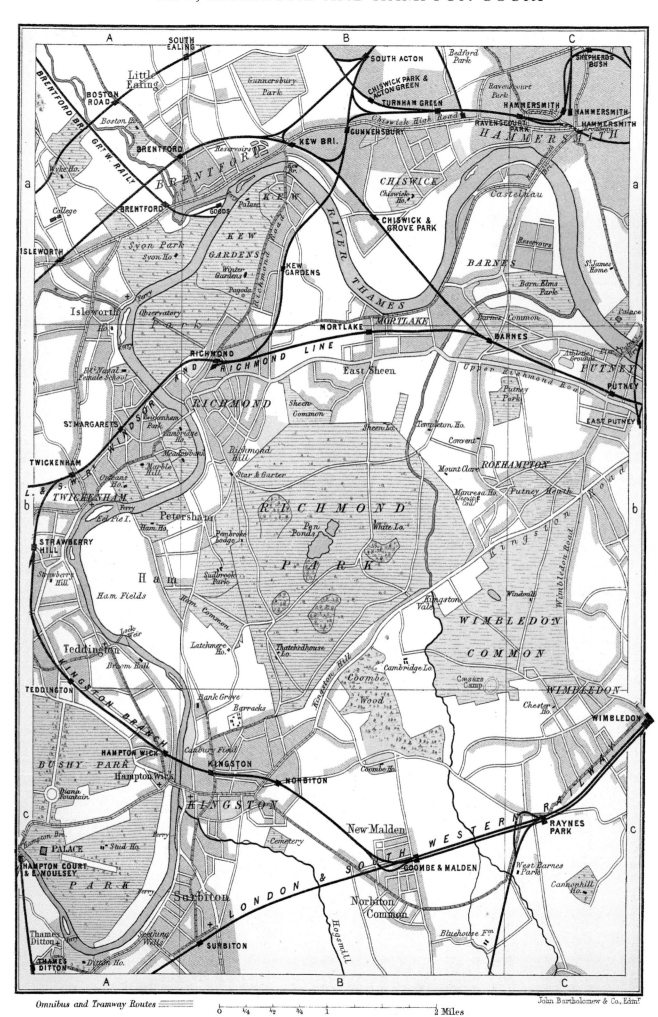

Omnibus and Tramway Routes ═══

0   ¼   ½   ¾   1   2 Miles

John Bartholomew & Co., Edin.

Plate No.   Plate No.   Plate No.

Plate 18.

THE THAMES TO WINDSOR

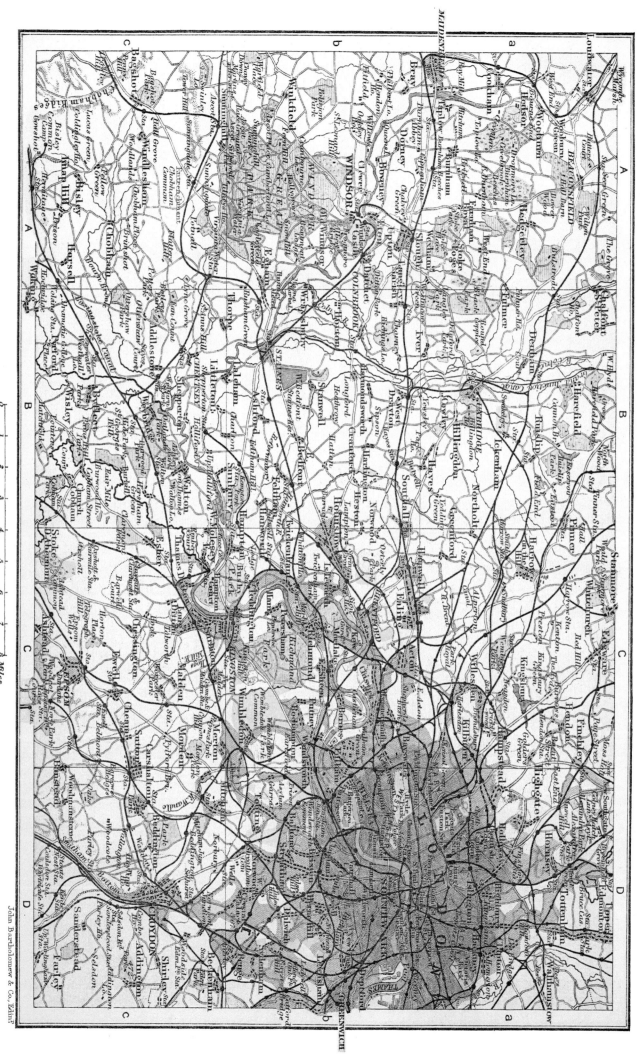

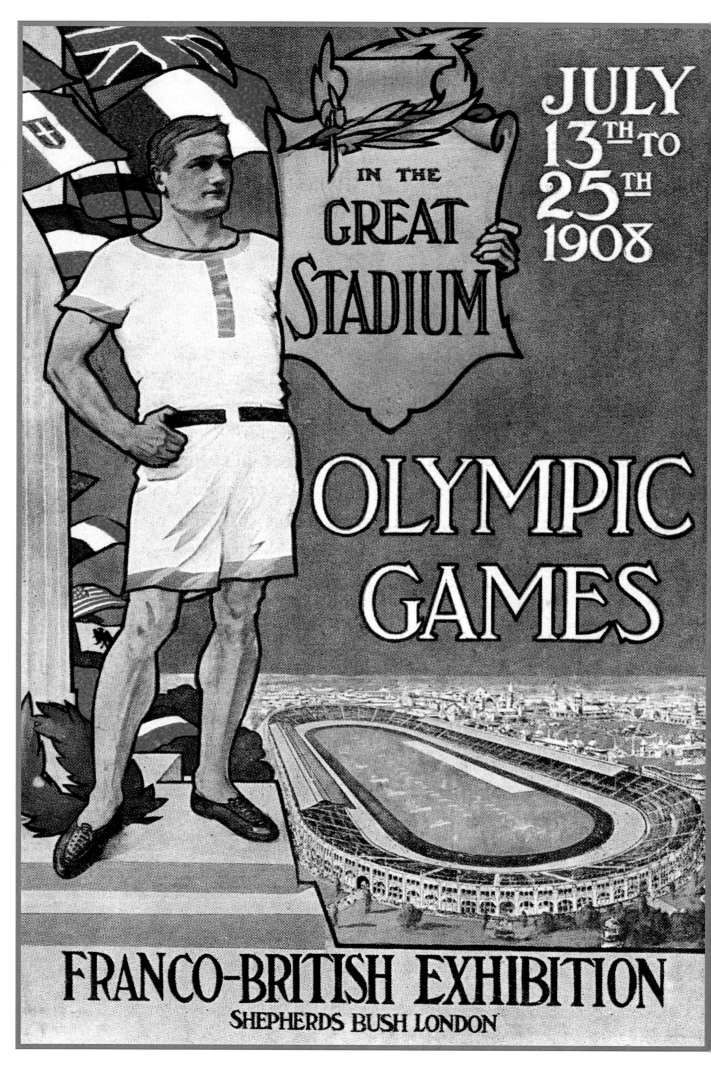

IN THE
GREAT
STADIUM

JULY
13TH TO
25TH
1908

OLYMPIC
GAMES

FRANCO-BRITISH EXHIBITION
SHEPHERDS BUSH LONDON

Three
LONDON 1908
THE RISE OF OLYMPISM

Cultures the world over have staged events throughout human history that focus on physical competition, celebrating both individual and collective achievement. The inspiration for the modern Olympics can, however, be traced to games first held nearly three thousand years ago near Mount Olympus in ancient Greece. Such events continued even after the civilization fell under Roman rule in 146BC following the Battle of Corinth but, in 394AD, the Games ceased. Considered a part of the then outlawed worship of false idols, sporting events were abolished under the orders of Emperor Theodosius I and the Olympic Games would have to wait for at least 1500 years before being revived.

During an international amateur congress on sport held at the Sorbonne, Paris in June 1894, the visionary Baron Pierre de Coubertin enthusiastically recommended the resurrection of the Greek Olympic Games. Coubertin, hailed by many as the father of the modern Games, believed that sport could exert a strong power capable of creating feelings of unity and peace among the many nations of the world, and came to believe that such a sense of togetherness could be fuelled with the revival of the Olympic Games.

An educationalist interested in the role of physical education and sport in schooling, it is widely thought that Coubertin drew his inspiration to pursue bringing about such a revival from the English public school system, and he indeed visited England to investigate educational methods first hand. He had long admired Thomas Arnold at Rugby School who, it is acknowledged, was the first educator to place emphasis on the importance of sporting competition in helping to educate the whole person; winning and losing being important in shaping a personality. Coubertin further believed that the poor physical condition of young French troops was largely to blame for his country's loss of the Franco-Prussian War of 1870 and was keen to not only rectify this deficiency but also explore the possibility of harnessing sporting competition to replace war, nurturing international tolerance, friendship and unity.

This ethos, allied to discoveries from excavations at the site of the ancient Greek Games at Olympia, kindling interest in the ancient use of sport to the same ends, meant he had therefore taken a keen interest in the Wenlock Olympian Society's annual games. These began in 1850 and were the brainchild of Dr. William Penny Brookes, a doctor and surgeon from Much Wenlock in the English county of Shropshire. Brookes, much like Coubertin, was also a believer in the values of antiquity and that a healthy body was as important as a healthy mind, with this synthesis forming the basis of his interest in the Games. In October 1890 Coubertin witnessed the Olympian Games, with its classical and traditional sports for amateur athletes, after accepting a written invitation from Dr. Brookes to attend. The two men discussed their similar

ambitions during the visit, with the doctor, aged eighty one, sharing his dream of an Olympic revival staged in Athens with the twenty seven year old Coubertin.

Dr William Penny Brookes.

On his return to France, Coubertin, inspired by his stay in Much Wenlock, sought to extend Brookes' idea. His new plans meant that Greece would not be the sole host, but the Games would be free to move to other cities and he referred warmly to his recent host's previous efforts to revive the Olympics of 1881 in a request made to the Greek authorities to that end. Coubertin was delighted when representatives from other countries participating in the congress agreed to his proposals. The decision to revive the Games was thereby made and the International Olympic Committee (IOC) founded. The congress representatives for Britain were the Prince of Wales - the future King Edward VII - and Arthur Balfour who would go on to become British Prime Minister.

The first modern Olympic Games were held in Athens in 1896, followed by Paris in 1900 and St. Louis in 1904. At the International Olympic Committee session held that same year it was proposed that 1908's Olympics be held in Rome. The British Olympic Association was founded at the House of Commons in 1905 as a direct result of this meeting, with William Henry Grenfell, later Lord Desborough, of Taplow Court as the Chairman.

A separate cycle of biennial Athenian games was also taking place around this time, with events held in the Greek capital in 1906 and also planned for 1910. Lord Desborough indeed attended in 1906 as the King's official representative, as well as participating as a member of a British fencing team. He returned with the view that the 1908 Olympic Games should be held in London as Rome playing host was now looking increasingly unlikely - the eruption of Mount Vesuvius in April 1906 had left Italy with pressing financial demands, any available funds being channelled into supporting disaster relief and rebuilding works.

Now Chairman of the British Olympic Association, and with the support of King Edward VIII, the dynamic Lord Desborough officially accepted the IOC's keenly anticipated invitation in November 1906 to step in and stage the Games in London following the Italian decision to withdraw. As well as relying on his own drive and determination, Lord

Desborough had also formed a close friendship with King Edward VIII, with the ensuing influence and support of the monarchy for the London Games soon to be witnessed in the staging of the event.

The size and scope of task ahead, especially considering the limited amount of time with which to organise the project, could not be underestimated. As well as coming up with facilities to stage the Games, there were also supporting administrative tasks, including standardising rules for the 22 different sports scheduled to take place, translating them into the languages of the 23 competing nations. Officials required to manage the events needed to be approached and formally invited to officiate. One such formal appointment is presented at the beginning of this book and shows the letter sent to William Barnard, his position described as Timekeeper for Marathon Race. Dated June 15th 1908, he had only until the 19th of June to accept as the full list of British officials had to be supplied to the British Olympic Council by that date. William would indeed go on to accept this responsibility as Senior Timekeeper for the Olympic Athletics programme.

It was fortunate that the Olympic year coincided with the planned opening of the Franco-British Exhibition to celebrate four years of the Entente Cordiale. In January 1907 work began on the 20 palaces and pavilions, 120 exhibition halls, various entertainment rides, waterways, bridges, pagodas and roads for the Franco-British Exhibition, and the organisers had also planned to build a stadium. The well-connected Lord Desborough seized the opportunity to persuade them to pay for a state of the art Olympic sporting stadium, as well as donating £2000 toward running costs.

In late July 1907 work began in the north east corner of the exhibition site. With little time to spare, the most advanced contemporary stadium and sports arena would have to be designed by engineer J.J. Webster and built by George Wimpey in less than 10 months. The oval arena featured a banked cycling track, a 586 yard running track, a state of the art 100 metre swimming and diving tank and platforms for wrestling and gymnastics at the centre, as well as an international assembly and dressing room complex. Additional information on the Great Stadium from the official 1908 Olympic Programme is also presented in this section.

Also featured is a letter compiled by Lord Desborough, dated 27th December 1907, appealing for funding for the 1908 Olympics. He had, much earlier, declared that the London Games were going to be the greatest Olympic Games ever, and was keen to live up to that promise. Up to that point, the modern Olympics was purely an amateur competition, with those wishing to enter able to simply turn up on the day and compete - they were not even required to participate under a national team or flag. Fewer competitors were entering the Games - the 1000 participants in Paris almost halving to 554 for the 1904 St. Louis Games, the vast majority of whom were American. Interest was waning and London was expected to raise the standard of the Games, to innovate and set a blueprint for the future.

Social fundraising functions had been arranged to which competitors and officials were to be invited, including a series of banquets. However, with only a few months to go, there was a genuine fear that the funding being attained would not be sufficient to deliver on the expectations and promises made. Lord Desborough's last paragraph of his letter spells out in no uncertain terms that the athletic world would expect a high standard to be set in this country, the birthplace of so many modern forms of athletics.

An approach was therefore made to Lord Northcliffe, a successful newspaper proprietor, to advertise publicly for Olympic funds. At first he was concerned that an association with the planned Games could damage his credibility should they turn out to be staged poorly. But, despite this reservation, he eventually agreed to Lord Desborough's appeal for funding, with it being published in the Daily Mail newspaper, which he had created in 1896 to much success and widespread popular appeal. Donations from the general public poured in, with amounts varying from 1 shilling up to the largest single sum of £1000.

Boosted by the support, the Great Stadium was duly completed and opened in April 1908. On May 26th of the same year King Edward VIII officially opened the stadium with the President of the French Republic in attendance. The programme is presented in this section, along with the details of an official pageant and procession for the day. Activities in the stadium had actually started on May 14th, and these are all presented and detailed in the republished "The Great Stadium – Guide and Sports Diary – May to October 1908".

The athletic events of the 1908 Games took place over two weeks in the Great Stadium, with the official opening on July 13th 1908 by King Edward VIII being notable as representatives from now organised national teams paraded for the first time in an Olympics opening ceremony. Also an innovation in the Olympic proceedings, gold, silver and bronze medals were to be presented to the winner, runner up and third-place finisher of each event respectively. The Sports Diary is followed by the republished official Programme of the 1908 Olympic Games of London 1908, the IV International Olympiad. However, it was the final event, one that took place on July 24th 1908, that stood out as the most eagerly awaited at the time and would go on to become one of the most iconic sporting spectacles of all time – the 1908 London Olympic Marathon.

Tom Sabin,
who won the 3 mile Bicycle Race in 1876, 1877 & 1878.

TAPLOW COURT,
TAPLOW,
BUCKS.

December 27th
1907.

Dear Sir,

In enclosing the accompanying
appeal for funds on behalf of the British
Olympic Council I should like to call attention
to the following facts.

(1) That during 1908 the Olympic Games
will be held in this country for the first time
since they were started in 1896.

(2) That as the International series of
Olympic Games takes place only every
four years, and as several countries desire
to hold them, a very long time will elapse
before they will again be celebrated in the
British Isles.

(3) That the Athletic World will expect a
High Standard to be set in this country, which is
the birthplace of so many modern forms of Athletics.

(4.) That the British Isles have a reputation
for hospitality to keep up, which cannot
be better exercised than on this occasion,
when representatives of some 22 countries
will be visiting us for the Olympic Games.
      A large sum of money will be required
for the following purposes:

(1) To defray the costs connected with carrying out
the lengthy programme, which, besides
including such sports as can take place
within the Stadium, will comprise such an
expensive item as an International Regatta
at Henley, and other events which cannot be
held at Shepherds Bush.

(2) To provide the Gold, Silver, and Bronze Medals,
the Diplomas and the Badges which will
amount to a very large sum.

(3.) To provide entertainment for the teams
of Foreign Athletes, who are expected to number

2000, the Judges. Members of the International Olympic Committee, the honorary Committees of various countries, and other distinguished visitors from abroad.

The idea of the Olympic Games is something above and beyond the mere holding of a great Athletic Meeting: the underlying hope is that the youth, and especially the Athletic youth of the different countries, by meeting each other in friendly rivalry, will get to know each other better, and appreciate each other more, and that they may take away the pleasantest recollections of the country which they may be seeing for the first time.

  With these ends in view I appeal with confidence to your generosity on this unique occasion —

    Yours truly <u>Desborough</u>

Franco-British Exhibition.

ROYAL AND PRESIDENTIAL

Opening

OF THE

Great Stadium

BY

HIS MAJESTY
KING EDWARD VII.

AND THE

PRESIDENT OF THE FRENCH REPUBLIC

M. ARMAND FALLIÈRES.

MAY 26th, 1903.

PROGRAMME

OF

ATHLETIC PAGEANT AND PROCESSION

OF OVER 1,000 ATHLETES, at 4.30,

Representing the various Athletic Sections of THE POLYTECHNIC, Regent Street, under the direction of ROBERT MITCHELL, Director of Education.

Order of Procession.

OLD ETON BLUES,
  J. E. K. STUDD (Cricket), V. R. HOARE (Cricket and Football), A. ARBUTHNOT (Rowing), who take an active part in the work of the Polytechnic.

THE ATHLETIC SECTIONS OF THE POLYTECHNIC, headed by their banners and emblems, and including National and International Champions.

  WOMEN'S GYMNASIUM.
  MEN'S GYMNASIUM.
  RUNNERS.
  FOOTBALL.
  CRICKET.
  BOXING.
  SWIMMING.
  ROWING.
  HOCKEY.
  LAWN TENNIS.

OLD QUINTINIANS' ATHLETIC CLUB.
TECHNICAL SCHOOL ATHLETIC CLUB.
ENGINEERING SCHOOL ATHLETIC CLUB.
ARCHITECTURAL SCHOOL ATHLETIC CLUB.
SECONDARY SCHOOL ATHLETIC CLUB.
  CYCLING.

In the Arena.

ATHLETIC TABLEAUX AND DISPLAY by members of the Polytechnic Gymnasia.

DIVING DISPLAY by the Amateur Diving Association.

WATER POLO MATCH—
  WESTON-SUPER-MARE S.C. (Champions of England) v. THE POLYTECHNIC (Champions of London, Middlesex, and the Southern Counties.

WRESTLING COMPETITION by members of the National Amateur Wrestling Association.

BOXING COMPETITION by Amateur Heavy-Weight Champions, 1906-1907, and other Champions.

1 MILE FLAT RACE, in which the French and English Champions will compete.

600 YARDS CYCLE RACE, all English Amateur Champions competing.

440 YARDS FLAT RACE.

5 MILES CYCLE RACE, all English Amateur Champions competing.

Director of the Sports - J. M. ANDREW, A.A.A., Hon. Sec. Polytechnic Harriers.

London, 13 July 1908. The Opening Ceremony of the Games of the IV Olympiad.

THE GREAT STADIUM.

GUIDE AND SPORTS DIARY.

[May to October—1908.]

In connection with the

FRANCO-BRITISH EXHIBITION,
SHEPHERDS BUSH,
LONDON ... W.

PRICE 1d.

THE GREAT STADIUM
AND
SPORT SECTION.

President:
THE LORD DESBOROUGH, C.V.O.
(President of the British Olympic Association.)

Commissioner General of the Franco=British Exhibition and The Stadium:
IMRE KIRALFY, Esq.

Director:
WILLIAM HENRY, Esq.
(Chief Secretary, Royal Life Saving Society and Member of the British Olympic Council.)

Sports Offices:—
THE STADIUM,
SHEPHERD'S BUSH,
LONDON, W.

SOME FACTS ABOUT THE STADIUM.

The Great Olympic Stadium, which has been provided at Shepherds Bush in connection with the Franco-British Exhibition for the promotion of Sport generally and the Olympic Games of 1908, is the largest and best appointed the world has yet known. It is capable of holding 60,000 people, nearly 20,000 of whom can be seated under cover, and contains dressing accommodation for over 2,000 competitors. It covers a space of about 1,000 by 700 feet and contains a banked cycle track of two-and-three-quarter laps to the mile, and a running track three laps to the mile. In the centre of one side and immediately opposite the Royal Box and other special enclosures, there is a swimming bath, 330 feet long, with a varying depth of 4 feet to 14 feet, in which the swimming, diving and water polo competitions will take place. The remainder of the arena inside the tracks is turfed, and measures about 700 feet by 300 feet.

The Sports commence 14th May and will finish at the end of October, the great Olympic Games taking place from 13th to 25th July; also from the 19th October. The Stadium is of easy access from all parts of London at small cost.

THE GREAT STADIUM
PRICES OF ADMISSION TO ATHLETIC & OTHER SPORTS
Except the Olympic Games and Fireworks.

Seats may be booked in advance.
SEE THE STADIUM GENERAL PLAN PAGE 20 & 21.

COVERED GRAND STAND—WEST.

Boxes (Holding 4)...16s. or 4s. per seat.
Block " M " to " Q " ... ... 3s. each.
Block " G " to " L " ... ... 2s. each.

COVERED GRAND STAND—EAST.

Boxes (Holding 4)...12s. or 3s. per seat.
Block " GG " to " MM " ... 2s. each.
Block " NN " to " SS " 1s. 6d. each.
Uncovered Seats ... ... 1s. each.
Standing Room in North and South
Stands ... ... 6d.

SEASON TICKETS ... 15s. each.

These Season Tickets will admit bearer on all occasions to the 1/- seats, except as stated above, and can only be booked through Secretaries of Athletic, Cycling, Swimming and kindred Clubs. Training Tickets will be granted to Season Ticket Holders only.

THURSDAY, MAY 14
THE DEDICATION CEREMONY.
FINCHLEY HARRIERS OPEN MEETING.

1. 100 Yards Open Invitation Scratch Race.
2. 100 ,, ,, Flat Handicap.
3. 300 ,, ,, ,, ,,
4. Half-Mile ,, ,, ,,
5. 2 Miles Open Walking Handicap.
6. 5 Miles Motor Cycle Handicap, Tourist Machines.
7. Half-Mile Open Cycle Handicap.
8. One Mile Open ,, First ,,
  In these events First Prizes will be of the guaranteed value of £4 4s., Seconds £2 2s., Thirds £1 1s.
9. 3 Miles Inter-Club Race (6 to enter, 4 to run, 3 to Count).
  First Team Prizes—Three Gold Medals. Second Team—Silver Medals.
10. Throwing the Discus.
  Open Competition (Free style).
11. Throwing the Javelin Open Competition (Free Style)
12. Tug-of-War.
First Prize, £2 2s. Seconds, £1 1s. Thirds, 10s. 6d.

NATIONAL AMATEUR WRESTLING ASSOCIA-TION CHAMPIONSHIPS.

12. 10st. 7lbs. Catch-as-Catch-Can.
13. Heavy Weights Catch-as-Catch-Can.
  (Diplomas and Gold and Silver Medals.

Entry Fees—Strangers—Nos. 1 to 8, 2s. each event ; No. 9 5s. per team ; Nos. 10 and 11, 1s. each event; Nos. 12 and 13, 2s. 6d. each event. Members, 1s. each event.

Entries close to C. R. Staines,
28, Broomhouse Road, Hurlingham, S.W.

SATURDAY, MAY 23
HIGHGATE HARRIERS OPEN MEETING

1. 100 Yards Open Flat Handicap
2. 100 ,, ,, ,, (6 yards limit)
3. 440 ,, ,, ,,
4. 880 ,, ,, ,,
5. One Mile ,, ,, ,,
6. One Mile Open Cycle ,,
7. One Lap Scratch Cycle Race
  Prizes value £5 5s., £2 2s , and £1 1s. in each event.
8. Three Miles Invitation Inter Club Team Race
  (or Relay Race)
  Prizes value £7 7s.

Entries with Fees—Flat events, 2s. for 1st event, and 1s. for each additional event ; Cycle events, 2s. for each event ; Club Members, 1s. any event. Close First Post Monday, May 18 (latest) to Hon. Sec. Highgate Harriers, G. E. Cackett, 81, Bedford Road, East Finchley, London. N.

NATIONAL AMATEUR WRESTLING CHAMPIONSHIP

10½ Stone, Cumberland and Westmorland Style.
Particulars of C. Quintana, 64, Claverton Street S.W.

AMATEUR FENCING CHAMPIONSHIPS
British Open Sabre Competitions.

MONDAY, MAY 25
SOUTHERN CYCLING UNION EVENING MEETING

1. Quarter Mile Cycle Handicap
2. One Mile Cycle Handicap
  (Open to Members of Affiliated Clubs).

WEDNESDAY, MAY 27
WEST END AMATEUR CYCLING ASSOCIATION

SATURDAY, MAY 30

AMATEUR ATHLETIC ASSOCIATION

Trial Races to select Representatives of Great Britain at the Olympic Games.

1. 100 Metres Flat Race (109.3 yards)
2. 200 ,, ,, ,, (218.6 ,,)
3. 400 ,, ,, ,, (437.2 ,,)
4. 800 ,, ,, ,, (874.4 ,,)
5. 1500 ,, ,, ,, (1639.5 ,,)
6. 110 ,. Hurdle Race (120.2 yards)
7. 400 ,, ,, ,, (437.2 ,,)
8. 3200 ,, Steeplechase (3497.6 ,,)
9. Standing Broad Jump
10. ,, High ,,
11. Running ,, ,,
12. ,, Broad ,,
13. Hop, Step and Jump
14. Pole Jump
15. Throwing the Hammer
16. Putting the Weight
17. Tug-of-War (Teams of eight)
18. 3500 Metres Walk (3825 Yards)
19. Discus (I.) Free style. (II.) As at Athens
20. Javelin (I.) Free style. (II.) With the Javelin held in the middle
21. Five Miles (8 Kilometres)

First Prize, Large Silver Medal. Second Prize, Small Silver Medal. Third Prize, Bronze Medal, in each event.

Entrance Fee for Each Competition, 5s. Entries, together with name of Club, Colours, and Entrance Fee, will be received up to Friday, 22nd May (after which no further entries can be received) by P. L. Fisher, Hon. Sec., 10, John Street, Adelphi, W.C. Telegraphic Address: "Athlete," London. The A.A.A. reserve the right to refuse and return any entry.

SATURDAY, MAY 16

QUEEN'S PARK HARRIERS

1. Two Miles Walking Handicap
2. 100 Yards Open Flat ,,
3. 300 ,, ,, ,,
4. 880 ,, ,, ,,
5. One Mile ,, ,,
6. 440 Yards ,, Cycle Handicap
7. 880 ,, ,, ,, ,,
8. 1000 Yards Members Flat Handicap
9. One Mile Relay Race (5 in a Team)
10. 9½ Stone Cumberland and Westmorland National Amateur Wrestling Association Championship.

Prizes value £7 for each event, except Member's Race in which prizes are value, £4 10s. and Wrestling Contests Prizes, value Six Guineas.

Entries with Fees 2s. for one Running event, 1s. each for others entered for; 2s. for One Cycling event, 3s. 6d. for Two. Close to W. Yexley, The Burlington Hotel, Burlington Road, Bayswater, last post Saturday, May 9. No late entry will be accepted.

WEDNESDAY, MAY 20

QUEEN'S PARK HARRIERS EVENING MEETING

POLYTECHNIC HARRIERS EVENING MEETING

WEST END AMATEUR CYCLING ASSOCIATION

SATURDAY, MAY 30

AMATEUR SWIMMING ASSOCIATION

Trial Water Polo Match North v South
Preliminary Diving Trials for Olympic Games.

Particulars from John C. Hurd, Hon Sec., 24, Cantley Avenue, Clapham, S.W.

MONDAY, JUNE 1.

RAILWAY CLEARING HOUSE A.C. ATHLETIC AND SWIMMING SPORTS.

WEDNESDAY, JUNE 3

FINCHLEY HARRIERS EVENING MEETING

1. One Mile Club Championship
2. 100 yards Handicap
3. 880 ,, ,,
4. 150 ,, Boys Handicap

PUTNEY ATHLETIC CLUB EVENING MEETING

5. Quarter Mile Cycle Handicap
6. One Mile ,, ,, for the Davis Cup
7. 150 yards Boy's Open Handicap for Lotinga Cup

SATURDAY, JUNE 6

AMATEUR SWIMMING ASSOCIATION

Trial Races and Competitions to select representatives of Great Britain at the Olympic Games.

1. 100 Metres race.
2. 200 ,, ,,
3. 400 ,, ,,
4. 1,500 ,, ,,
5. 100 ,, Back Swimming Race.
6. 200 ,, Breast ,, ,,
7. High Diving. [Continued over

8   Graceful Diving.
9.   Water Polo Match—England *v.* a combined team selected from Scotland, Ireland and Wales. Competitors selected by the Association.

NATIONAL PHYSICAL RECREATION SOCIETY'S CHAMPIONSHIPS

AMATEUR FENCING ASSOCIATION
British Epee Championships.

NATIONAL AMATEUR WRESTLING ASSOCIATION CHAMPIONSHIPS

Heavy-weight, Cumberland and Westmorland style.

8½st. Catch-as-Catch-can.

Particulars of C. Quintana. Hon. Sec., 64, Claverton St., N.W.

MONDAY, JUNE 8 (Whit Monday)

POLYTECHNIC SPORTS FESTIVAL

(Under the management of the Polytechnic Harriers, Cycling, Swimming, Boxing and Gymnastic Clubs.

ATHLETICS.

1.   3 Miles Open Scratch race.
2.   440 Yards ,,   ,,   ,,
3.   100 Yards Open Handicap.
4.   880   ,,   ,,   ,,

[Continued over

5   2 Miles Open Walking Handicap.
Value of prizes for events 1 and 2 £7 7s., £2 2s., £1 1s., 3 and 4 £5 5s., £2 2s., £1 10s. 6d. and No. 5, £4 4s., £2 12s. 6d., £1 1s and 10s. 6d.

CYCLING.
6.   Quarter Mile Open Handicap.
7.   One   ,,   ,,   ,,
8.   Five Miles Open Scratch Race.
Value of prizes 6 and 7 £5, £2, and £1, and for No. 8 £6 6s., £2 2s. and £1 1s. and two lap prizes.

SWIMMING.
One length (100 Metres) open handicap.   Prizes
9.   value £5, £2 10s, £1, 15s. 10s., and 5s.
10.   Exhibition High and Fancy Diving (Invitation).
11.   Fancy Costume Race for Members.
12.   Water Polo.   Polytechnic and Rest of London Seven prices value 10s. each.
13.   Comic Race for Members.

BOXING.
14.   Open Boxing Tournament, 9st. 6lb. by Invitation.   Prize value £6 6s.

GYMNASTICS.
15   Massed Drill by Polytechnic Gymnastic (Ladies and Men).

Entry Fees.—Events 1 to 5 Non-Members, 2s. each or 3s. 6d. for two Events.   Members 1s. 6d each or 2s. 6d. for two events.   Events 6 and 7 Non-Members 1s. 6d. each.   Members 1s. each.   Event 8, Non-Members 2s. 6d. Members, 2s.   Event 9 Non-Members 3s., Members 1s. 6d., 11 and 13, 6d. each event.   Entries close first post June 1st. to J. M. Andrew, Sports Hon. Sec., 309, Regent Street, London, W.

SATURDAY, JUNE 13

ESSEX BEAGLES OPEN MEETING
1.   100 yards Flat Handicap
2.   Half Mile Open Cycle Handicap
3.   880 yards Open Flat   ,,
4.   Ten Miles Motor Cycle   ,,
5.   One Mile Open Cycle   ,,
6.   220 yards Open Flat   ,,
7.   Two Miles Open Walking Handicap
8.   One Mile Members Handicap

Prizes in events 1, 3, 6, and 7 value £4, £1 10s., and 15s; on events 2 and 6 value £5, £2 and 15s; and in event 4, value £5 5s., £2, and £1.

Particulars as to closing of entries from F. A. Downes, Jnr., 180, Upton Lane, Forest Gate.

HOLLOWAY UNITED SWIMMING CLUB
1.   66 yards Open Handicap
2.   66   ,,   Ladies' Open Handicap
3.   66   ,,   Club Handicap
4.   Water Polo Match
5.   220 yards Club Junior Championship
Prizes for event 1, value £7; for event 2, £3; for event 3, £1 10s.; for event 4, £1.

Also display of Diving.   Particulars as to closing of entries, &c., from Messrs. C. F. Simpson and R. H. Hassell, 49, Crayford Road, Holloway, N.

WEDNESDAY, JUNE 17

QUEEN'S PARK HARRIERS EVENING MEETING

POLYTECHNIC HARRIERS EVENING MEETING

SATURDAY, JUNE 20

PUTNEY, PADDINGTON, & POLYTECHNIC CYCLING CLUBS.

(Great Joint Cycling v Athletic Festival).

OPEN CYCLE EVENTS.

1.   440 Yards Handicap
2.   Mile Open Handicap
   Prizes for each event, value £5, £2, £1 and 10s.
3.   Five Miles Scratch Race
4.   One Lap Open Scratch Race
Prizes for each event, value £7, £2, £1 and 10s. and Lap Prizes for No. 3
5.   Mile Team Race Championship of London.

Entry Fees.—1s. 6d. each Handicap and 2s. 6d. each Scratch Race.   For all Members of Promoting Clubs, 1s. each Handicap and 2s. each Scratch Race.

OPEN FLAT EVENTS.
1.   100 Yards Open Handicap
2.   880   ,,   ,,   ,,
3.   2 Mile Open Walking Handicap
   Prizes value £4, £2, £1 and 10s for each event.

Entry Fees—1s. 6d. each event.

Entries close 1st Post, Monday, June 15th, to R. J. Gear, 309, Regent Street, W.

AMATEUR SWIMMING CLUB RACES

Club Championship, Diving Display and Water polo match Amateur v Hornsey.

WEDNESDAY, JUNE 24

LONDON UNITED TRAMWAYS SPORTS
11 a.m. to 8 p.m.
OPEN EVENTS.

1. Hurdle Race.
2. Two Miles Walking Race.
3. Two Miles Cycle Race.
4. Half Mile Cycle Race.
5. 100 Yards Flat Handicap.
6. 440 Yards Flat Handicap.
7. Motor Cycle or Motor Paced Race.
8. Tug of War for the Lady Robinson Challenge Cup, open to all Tramway Teams in the United Kingdom.

Also numerous Club events and Tugs of War for the Clifton Robinson Challenge Cup and Shield.

Particulars of W. G. Murrin, 88, High Rd. Chiswick.

WEST-END AMATEUR CYCLING ASSOCIATION

SATURDAY, JUNE 27

NATIONAL CYCLIST'S UNION CHAMPIONSHIPS

1. Quarter Mile Amateur Championship.
2. One Mile Amateur Championship.
3. Five Miles Amateur Championship.
4. One Mile Open Handicap.

Particulars of H. R. Noble, Sec. N C U., 57, Chancery Lane, E C.

ZEPHYR SWIMMING CLUB OPEN MEETING

1. 66 Yards Club Handicap.
2. 66 Yards Gentlemen's Open Handicap.
3. 66 Yards Ladies' Open Handicap.
4. Water Polo Competition.
5. Open Diving Competition.

Particulars of W. Jackson, Hon. Sec, 39, Upper Marylebone Street, W.

MONDAY, JULY 6

PUTNEY ATHLETIC CLUB EVENING MEETING

1. One Mile Cycle Championship of Club for the "Kimber" Cup.

2. Twenty-five Miles Cycle Championship of Club and Sealed Handicap.

WEDNESDAY, JULY 8

POLYTECHNIC HARRIERS EVENING MEETING

THURSDAY & FRIDAY, JULY 9 & 10
From 11 a m. to 6 p m.

THE ELEVENTH INTERNATIONAL FLY AND BAIT CASTING TOURNAMENT

23 Competitions open to Amateurs and All Comers.

For Rules and Conditions, see *"Fishing Gazette,"* May 2, 1908.

Particulars of J. T. Emery, Hon. Sec. to the Committee of Management, 15, Atherton Rd., Forest Gate, London, E.

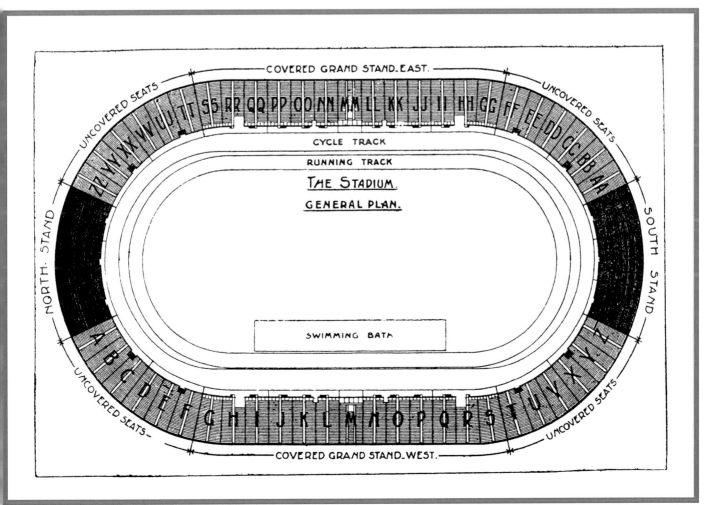

SATURDAY, JULY 11

THE POLYTECHNIC OPEN MEETING

Polytechnic Harriers v Le Stade Francais.

1. 100 Yards Flat
2. 440 ,, ,,
3. 1 Mile Flat
4. 3 ,, ,,
5. 120 Yards Hurdle
6. High Jump
7. Long ,,

Open Athletic Handicaps.

8. 120 Yards Flat
9. 880 ,, ,,
10. 120 ,, Hurdle
11. 2 Miles Walking
12. ¼ ,, Flat
13. 3 ,, ,,

Prizes for events 1 to 8, Gold and Silver Medals; events 9 and 10, value £9 9s. each; event 11, £7; event 12, £8 10s.; events 13 and 14, £10 10s. each; 15 and 16, £8 8s., 17 and 18, £10 each.

Cycling Events.

14. ¼ Mile Cycling
15. 1 ,, ,,
16. ½ Mile Scratch Cycling
17. 5 ,, ,, ,,

Prizes for events 15 and 16, value £8 8s each; for 17 and 18, £10 each.

Swimming.

18. 1 Length Open Handicap
19. Men's Open Team Race
20. Water Polo Tournament

Prizes for event 18 value £5; event 19, value £4; event 20, value £7 4s 6d.

Open Boxing Tournament—10st. 4lb.
Prize, Silver Cup.

Particulars of J. M. Andrew, Hon. Sec., 309, Regent Street, W.

THE OLYMPIC GAMES
LONDON 1908

Will take place Daily in

THE GREAT STADIUM

Shepherd's Bush, W.

From the 13th to the 25th July.

Morning from 10 a.m. Afternoon from 2.30 p.m.

ADMISSION FROM 1/- to 21/-

Serial Tickets for the whole of the Games in the Stadium from **£1 10s.** to **£12 12s.**

WEEKLY SERIAL TICKETS HALF-PRICE.

Now on sale at all the Principal Agencies and Libraries.

Letters relating to the sale of Tickets must be addressed to the **Secretary, Ticket Department, Franco-British Exhibition, Shepherd's Bush, London, W.,** and marked "Olympic Games."

Letters relating to the Programmes of the Olympic Games should be addressed to the Hon. Secretary, British Olympic Association, 108, Victoria Street, London, S W.

THE OLYMPIC GAMES

Events in the Stadium

FIRST WEEK, JULY 13 TO 18

Morning - From 10 a.m.   Afternoon - From 2.30 p.m.

13th, OPENING CEREMONY.

		h. m.		h. m.
14.	Field Athletics	3 0	Field Athletics 3 30
	Track Athletics	1 30	Track Athletics ... 1 30
	Cycling	0 30	Cycling 2 15
	Gymnastics	4 0	Gymnastics ... 4 0
	Swimming & Diving	2 30	Swimming & Diving ... 2 30
15.	Field Athletics	3 0	Field Athletics ... 3 30
	Track Athletics	2 0	Track Athletics ... 2 30
	Cycling	2 30	Cycling 1 10
	Gymnastics	4 0	Gymnastics ... 4 0
	Swimming & Diving	2 30	Swimming, Diving & Water Polo ... 2 30
16.	Field Athletics	3 0	Field Athletics ... 3 30
	Track Athletics	2 0	Track 2 30
	Cycling	2 30	Cycling 1 10
	Gymnastics	4 0	Gymnastics ... 4 0
	Swimming & Diving	2 30	Swimming, Diving & Water Polo ... 2 30
17.	Field Athletics	3 0	Field Athletics ... 3 30
	Archery	4 0	Track Athletics ... 1 30
	Swimming	2 30	Cycling 1 40
			Swimming, Diving & Water Polo ... 2 30
18.	Field Athletics	3 0	Field Athletics ... 3 30
	Track Athletics	1 0	Track Athletics ... 2 0
	Archery	4 0	Cycling 2 50
	Swimming & Diving	2 30	Swimming, Diving & Water Polo ... 2 30

SECOND WEEK, JULY 20 TO 25

THE OLYMPIC GAMES

Events in the Stadium

Morning—From 10 a.m.   Afternoon—From 2.30 p.m.

20.	Field Athletics	3 0	Field Athletics 3 30
	Archery	2 30	Track Athletics .. 1 30
	Swimming & Diving	2 30	Swimming & Diving ... 2 30
	Wrestling	3 0	Wrestling 3 0
[21.	Field Athletics	3 0	Field Athletics ... 3 30
	Swimming & Diving	2 30	Track Athletics ... 1 30
	Wrestling	3 0	Swimming & Diving ... 2 30
			Wrestling ... 3 0
22.	Field Athletics	3 0	Field Athletics ... 3 30
	Swimming & Diving	2 30	Track Athletics ... 1 30
	Wrestling	3 0	Swimming, Diving, & Water Polo ... 2 30
			Wrestling 3 0
23.	Field Athletics	3 0	Field Athletics ... 3 30
	Swimming & Diving	2 30	Track Athletics ... 1 30
	Wrestling	3 0	Swimming, Diving, & Water Polo ... 2 30
			Wrestling 3 0
24.	Field Athletics	3 0	Field Athletics ... 3 30
	Swimming & Diving	2 30	Track Athletics ... 1 30

MARATHON RACE.

	Wrestling	3 0	Swimming, Diving & Water Polo... 2 30
			Wrestling 3 0
25.	Field Athletics	3 0	Field Athletics ... 3 30
	Swimming & Diving	2 30	Track Athletics ... 1 0
	Wrestling	3 0	Swimming, Diving & Water Polo... 2 30

MARATHON RACE.
FRIDAY AFTERNOON JULY 24.

Price of Tickets for the Olympic Games in the Stadium.
13th to 25th July.

GRAND STAND WEST. (near the Royal Box and other special enclosures).

(SEE PLAN PAGES 20 & 21.)

	Opening & Closing Days.			Regular Afternoons.			Fore-noons.			Serial Tickets for the whole of the games in the Stadium on 23 Test Meetings.		
	£	s.	d.	£	s.	d.	£	s.	d.	£	s.	d.
Boxes (holding 4)	8	8	0	4	4	0	2	2	0	50	8	0
Block G H I. ...First 15 rows ...	0	15	0	0	7	6	0	3	6	4	4	0
Remaining rows ...	0	10	0	0	5	0	0	2	6	3	3	0
Block J K L ...First 14 rows ...	1	1	0	0	10	6	0	5	0	6	6	0
Remaining rows ...	0	10	0	0	5	0	0	2	6	3	3	0
Block M ...First 7 rows ...	2	2	0	1	1	0	0	10	6	12	12	0
Next 10 rows	1	1	0	0	10	0	0	5	0	6	6	0
Next 6 rows ...	0	15	0	0	7	6	0	3	6	4	4	0
Next 3 rows ...	0	10	0	0	5	0	0	2	6	3	3	0
Block N O P ...First 4 rows ...	2	2	0	1	1	0	0	10	6	12	12	0
Next 15 rows ...	1	1	0	0	10	6	0	5	0	6	6	0
Next 6 rows ...	0	15	0	0	7	6	0	3	6	4	4	0
Next 3 rows ...	0	10	0	0	5	0	0	2	6	3	3	0
Block Q R S ...First 5 rows ...	2	2	0	1	1	0	0	10	6	12	12	0
Next 14 rows ...	1	1	0	0	10	6	0	5	0	6	6	0
Next 6 rows ...	0	15	0	0	7	6	0	3	6	4	4	0
Next 3 rows ...	0	10	0	0	5	0	0	2	6	3	3	0

Weekly Serial Tickets half-price to be obtained from the Ticket Dept. Shepherd's Bush and all Ticket Agents.

Price of Tickets for the Olympic Games in the Stadium.
13th to 25th July.

GRAND STAND EAST.

(SEE PLAN PAGES 20 & 21.)

		Opening & Closing Days.			Regular Afternoons.			Fore-noons.			Serial Tickets for the whole of the games in the Stadium or 23 Test Meetings.		
Boxes (holding 4)		4	4	0	2	2	0	1	1	0	25	4	0
Block GG HH for the Competitors & Officials													
Block II.	First 19 rows ...	0	10	0	0	5	0	0	2	6	3	3	
	Remaining rows ...	0	6	0	0	3	0	0	1	6	2	2	0
Block JJ KK LL.	First 19 rows ...	0	10	0	0	5	0	0	2	6	3	3	0
	Remaining rows ...	0	6	0	0	3	0	0	1	6	2	2	0
Block MM.	First 17 rows ...	0	10	0	0	5	0	0	2	6	3	3	0
	Remaining rows ...	0	6	0	0	3	0	0	1	6	2	2	0
Block NN OO PP.	First 19 rows ...	0	10	0	0	5	0	0	2	6	3	3	0
	Remaining rows ...	0	6	0	0	3	0	0	1	6	2	2	0
Block QQ RR SS.	First 19 rows ...	0	8	0	0	4	0	0	2	0	2	12	6
	Remaining rows ...	0	6	0	0	3	0	0	1	6	2	2	0
Uncovered Seats.	A to F	0	4	0	0	2	0	0	1	0	1	10	0
	T U V ...	0	10	0	0	5	0	0	2	6	3	3	0
	X Y Z ...	0	6	0	0	3	0	0	1	6	2	2	0
	AA BB CC ...	0	6	0	0	3	0	0	1	6	2	2	0
	DD EE FF ...	0	8	0	0	4	0	0	2	0	2	12	
	TT to ZZ ...	0	4	0	0	2	0	0	1	0	1	10	
Uncovered for standing		0	2	0	0	1	0	0	0	6			

Weekly Serial Tickets half-price to be obtained from the Ticket Dept. Shepherd's Bush and all Ticket Agents.

The Olympic Games outside the Stadium and the dates of commencing are as follows:—

April. Racquets and Tennis at Queen's Club.

June 1. Golf at Sandwich and Deal.

„ 15. Polo at Hurlingham.

July 6. Lawn Tennis at Wimbledon.

„ 16. Fencing in special enclosure adjoining Stadium.

„ 8. Shooting at Bisley.

„ 8. Clay-Bird Shooting at Uxendon School.

„ 11. Motor-Boat Racing in Southampton Water.

„ 27. Yacht Racing at Ryde.

„ 28. Olympic Regatta at Henley.

Oct. 19. Figure Skating at Prince's Rink.

---◆---

The Winter Section of the Olympic Games at the Stadium will commence October 19, and will include Rugby and Association Football, Hockey, Lacrosse, and Boxing.

The offices of the British Olympic Association are at
108, Victoria Street, London, S.W.

SATURDAY, AUGUST 15

POLYTECHNIC, PUTNEY & PADDINGTON CYCLING CLUB

(Great Joint Cycling and Athletic Festival)
The Meeting of "The 3 Ps"

OPEN CYCLING EVENTS.
1. 440 Yards Open Handicap
2. 1 Mile Open Handicap
3. 5 „ Scratch Race
4. 1 Lap Open Scratch Race

Prizes value £5, £2, £1 and 10s. for Events 1 and 2, and value £7, £2, £1 and 10s. for Events 3 and 4, also Lap Prizes for Event 3.

Entry Fees.—1s. 6d. each Handicap and 2s. 6d. each Scratch Race. For all Members of the Promoting Clubs, 1s. each Handicap and 2s. each Scratch Race.

OPEN FLAT EVENTS.
1. 100 Yards Open Handicap
2. 880 „ „ „
3. 2 Mile Open "Walking" Handicap

Prizes value £4, £2, £1 and 10s., for each Event.

Entry Fees.—1s. 6d. each Event.

Entries close 1st Post, Monday, 10th August, to R. J. Gear, 309, Regent Street, W.

AMATEUR DIVING ASSOCIATION DISPLAY

CITY OF WESTMINSTER SWIMMING CLUB CHAMPIONSHIP

WEDNESDAY AUGUST 19

QUEEN'S PARK HARRIERS' EVENING MEETING

SATURDAY, AUGUST 22

AUTO CYCLE UNION SPORTS
1. One Mile Time Trial
2. One Hour Scratch Race
3. Five Miles Handicap
4. Five Miles Tourist Handicap

Particulars of F. Straight, 18, Down Street, Piccadilly

ST. MARTIN'S HARRIER'S SPORTS

OPEN EVENTS.
1. 100 Yards Handicap
2. 300 „ „
3. 880 „ „
4. 2 Miles Walking Handicap
5. 100 Yards Hurdle „

POSTAL EVENTS.
6. 100 Yards Handicap
7. 440 „ „
8. 150 „ Veteran's Handicap
9. Mile Running Championship
10. 5 Miles Cycling Championship

ST. MARTIN'S SWIMMING CLUB
1. 100 Yards Swimming Handicap
*2. 880 „ „ Championship

* Championship of the Postal Service.
Particulars of C. Robson, Inland Section, General Post Office, E.C.

AMATEUR DIVING ASSOCIATION DISPLAY

WEDNESDAY: AUGUST 26
POLYTECHNIC CYCLING CLUB EVENING MEETING

SATURDAY, AUGUST 29

NATIONAL CYCLISTS UNION (London Centre) CHAMPIONSHIPS

1. One Mile Championship, National Cyclists' Union (London Centre). Prize, Gold Medal.
2. Ten Miles Championship, National Cyclists' Union (London Centre). Prize, Gold Medal.
3. Two Miles Tandem Championship, National Cyclists Union (London Centre). Prizes, Gold Medals.

In each of the above Championships, Silver Medals will be offered to all riders beating time Standard to be fixed on the day of the race.

Entry Fee.—2s. 6d. each rider, each event.
4. One Lap Cycle Handicap.
5. Half Mile Cycle Handicap,
Prizes value £5, £2 and £1 each event.

Entry Fee, 2s. each rider, each event.

Entries close 1st post Monday, August 24th to A. J. Wakeford, Hon. Sec., London Centre, 267, Clapham Road, London, S.W.

AMATEUR DIVING ASSOCIATION DISPLAY

SATURDAY AUGUST 29

UNITED HARRIERS' SPORTS.
1. 100 Yards Open Handicap
2. 300 „ „ „
3. 880 „ „ „
4. Four Miles Walking Handicap
5. 220 Yards Members „
6. One Mile Walking „

Continued over

WRESTLING COMPETITION

10 st. Catch-as-catch-can

Particulars of H. W. Keen, 22, Canonbury Road, N.

ACTON SWIMMING CLUB

Events

1. 100 Yards Open Handicap for men
2. 100 ,,   ,,   ,, for ladies
3. 50 ,, Members ,,
4. Team Race Handicap
5. Polo Match

Particulars of A. C. Kirbright, 5, Mansell Road, Acton, W.

WEDNESDAY, SEPTEMBER 2

FINCHLEY HARRIERS EVENING MEETING

1. Half-Mile Club Championship.
2. 150 Yards Veterans' Handicap.
3. 440 Yards Handicap.
4. 120 Yards Boys' Handicap.

SATURDAY, SEPTEMBER 5

LONDON SCHOOLS SWIMMING ASSOCIATION

Swimming and Life Saving Championships and Childrens' Day at the Stadium.

Grand Display by Members of the Amateur Diving Association.

SATURDAY, SEPTEMBER 11 & 12

MIDDLESEX WALKING CLUB

TWENTY-FOUR HOURS AMATEUR RECORD RACE.

A Similar event has not been held for 27 years.

Particulars of Mr. J. Barnes Moss, 4, Shakespeare Road, Acton.

SHEPHERDS BUSH S.C.

SWIMMING, DIVING AND WATER POLO SPORTS.

WEDNESDAY, SEPTEMBER 16

QUEEN'S PARK HARRIERS EVENING MEETING

SATURDAY, SEPTEMBER 19

RANELAGH HARRIERS' ATHLETIC SPORTS

GREAT FIREWORK DISPLAYS
IN THE STADIUM.

Alternately,

By Messrs. JAS. PAIN & SONS of London,
and
Messrs. RUGGIERI of Paris.

EVERY TUESDAY, THURSDAY AND SATURDAY.

Prices of Admission to Seats for the Firework Displays

COVERED GRAND STAND—WEST.

Boxes (Holding 4)	£1 or 5/- per seat
Block G to L First 18 rows ...	... 2/6 each
Remaining rows ...	... 2/- ,,
Central Block M Front seats ...	... 3/- ,,
Upper ,, ...	... 2/6 ,,
Blocks N O P Q R S Front seats	... 2/6 ,,
Upper ,,	... 2/- ,,
Uncovered Seats A B C and X Y Z	... 1/- ,,
D E F and T U V	... 1/6 ,,
Admission to North and South Stand	... 6d. ,,

FRANCO-BRITISH EXHIBITION, 1908.

SHEPHERD'S BUSH, ... LONDON, W.

Open May to October.

The Greatest Exhibition ever held in London, Demonstrating to the World the Products and Resources of the British Empire, and of France and her Colonies.

RELATIVE AREAS OF EXHIBITIONS.

Great Exhibition in London, 1851—21 acres, 16 acres buildings. International Exhibition, London, 1862—23½ acres, 16¾ acres buildings. **Franco-British Exhibition, 1908.**—140 acres, over 40 acres buildings.

The best British and French Military Bands will perform daily. The Pleasure Gardens contain the **most novel** and **refined attractions** ever presented in London.

Fireworks Tuesdays, Thursdays and Saturdays. Grounds Illuminated daily. Great Sports Meetings in the Stadium.

Season Tickets—For Ladies and Gentlemen £1 1s. each. For Children under twelve, 10s. 6d. each. Now on sale at all the principal agencies and Libraries.

Excursions from all parts of the United Kingdom and the Continent

Admission 1/-

OLYMPIC GAMES

OF

LONDON, 1908

IV. INTERNATIONAL OLYMPIAD

PROGRAMME

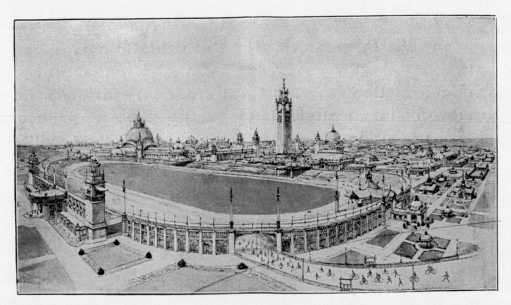

VIEW OF STADIUM

BRITISH OLYMPIC COUNCIL

Chairman—THE RIGHT HON. LORD DESBOROUGH OF TAPLOW

Offices—108 Victoria Street, Westminster, London, S.W.

OLYMPIC GAMES

OF

LONDON, 1908

IV. INTERNATIONAL OLYMPIAD

PROGRAMME

This Programme contains the proposals of the British Olympic Council as sanctioned by the International Olympic Committee at their Meeting at The Hague, May, 1907.

It is sent out in order to give the Athletic and Sporting Associations of different countries the opportunity of making suggestions for the final draft. It will be difficult to make any large alterations in the present proposals, but all suggestions sent in before July, 1907, will be very carefully considered.

COUNCIL

OF

BRITISH OLYMPIC ASSOCIATION.

Chairman : Rt. Hon. LORD DESBOROUGH of Taplow, President of the Epée Club ; Acting President, Royal Life Saving Society ; Member of the International Olympic Committee.

Rt. Hon. LORD MONTAGU of Beaulieu, Automobile Club.

Col. Sir C. E. HOWARD VINCENT, K.C.M.G., C.B., A.D.C. to the King, M.P., Member of International Olympic Committee.

Sir LEES KNOWLES, Bart., Ex-President, Cambridge University Athletic Club.

H. BENJAMIN, Esq., Ex-President, Amateur Swimming Association.

T. W. J. BRITTEN, Esq., Hon. Treas., National Cyclists Union.

W. HAYES FISHER, Esq., President, National Skating Association.

R. G. GRIDLEY, Esq., Hon. Sec., Amateur Rowing Association.

G. ROWLAND HILL, Esq., President, Rugby Football Union.

P. L. FISHER, Esq., Hon. Sec., Amateur Athletic Association.

Capt. A. HUTTON, F.S.A., President, Amateur Fencing Association.

E. LAWRENCE LEVY, Esq., Hon. Sec., Amateur Gymnastic Association.

E. SYERS, Esq., Hon. Sec., Figure Skating Club.

F. J. WALL, Esq., Hon. Sec., Football Association.

Col. H. WALROND, Hon. Sec., Royal Toxophilite Society.

THEODORE A. COOK, Esq., F.S.A., Amateur Fencing Association.

H. M. TENNENT, Esq., Hon. Sec., Hockey Association.

Maj.-Gen. Rt. Hon. LORD CHEYLESMORE, C.V.O., Chairman of Council, National Rifle Association.

Col. G. M. ONSLOW, Hon. Sec., National Physical Recreation Society.

W. HENRY, Esq., Hon. Sec., Royal Life Saving Society.

G. S. ROBERTSON, Esq., British Representative Juror in Olympic Games of Athens, 1906.

GUY M. CAMPBELL, Esq,, F.R.G.S.

Major EGERTON GREEN, Hurlingham Club.

F. B. O. HAWES, Esq., Hon. Sec., Lacrosse Union.

A. H. SUTHERLAND, Esq., Chairman, Amateur Wrestling Association.

G R. MEWBURN, Esq., Hon. Sec., Lawn Tennis Association.

J. BLAIR, Esq., Scottish Cyclists Union.

D. S. DUNCAN, Esq., Hon. Sec., Scottish Amateur Athletic Association.

MICHAEL J. BULGER, Esq., M.D., Irish Amateur Athletic Association.

W. RYAN RICHARDSON, Esq., Hon. Sec., Amateur Golf Championship Committee.

Rev. R. S. DE COURCY LAFFAN, *Hon. Sec.,* Member of International Olympic Committee.

PROGRAMME.

ATHLETICS.	Maximum No. of Competitors from each Country
100 metres Flat (109·3 yards).	**12**
200 metres Flat (218·6 yards).	**12**
400 metres Flat (437·2 yards).	**12**
800 metres Flat (874·4 yards).	**12**
1,500 metres Flat (1,639·5 yards)	**12**
110 metres Hurdle (120·2 yards).	**12**
400 metres Hurdle (437·2 yards).	**12**
3,200 metres Steeplechase (3,497·6 yards).	**12**
5 miles Run (8·047 kilometres).	**12**
10 miles Walk (16 kilometres).	**12**
Marathon Race (25 miles) (40 kilometres).	**12**

ATHLETICS—continued.	
Standing Broad Jump.	12
Standing High Jump.	12
Running Broad Jump.	12
Running High Jump.	12
Hop, Step, and Jump.	12
Pole Jump.	12
Hammer.	12
Shot.	12
Tug-of-War.	4 teams
3 Mile Team Race (4·8 kilometres). (5 to run, 3 to count.)	1 team
3,500 Metres Walk (3,825 yards).	12
Discus. I. Free style. II. Greek style.	12 12
Javelin.	12

ARCHERY.

	Maximum No. of Competitors from each Country
Gentlemen.—The York Round. 72 arrows at 100 yards (91·4 metres), 48 arrows at 80 yards (73 metres), 24 arrows at 60 yards (54·8 metres).	**30**
Ladies.—The National Round. 48 arrows at 60 yards (54·8 metres), 24 arrows at 50 yards (45·7 metres).	**30**
Gentlemen. 40 arrows at 50 metres (54·6 yards), shot singly Continental fashion.	**30**

CYCLING.

Bicycle.

One lap (640 yards = 585 metres).	**12**
1,000 metres (1,093·6 yards).	**12**
5,000 metres (5,468 yards).	**12**
20 kilometres (12·4 miles).	**12**
100 kilometres (62 miles).	**12**
Pursuit Race. 1 mile (1·6 kilometres). Teams of four to start. First three to count in each heat.	**1 team**

Tandem Bicycle.

2,000 metres (1·24 miles).	**6 pairs**

FENCING.

I. Epee.

A. Individual.

12

B. International Teams of 8.

1 team

II. Sabre.

A. Individual.

12

B. International Teams of 8.

1 team

III. Foils.

A display (with commemorative medals for all engaged) by picked amateurs of all nations.

FOOTBALL (ASSOCIATION).

4 teams

FOOTBALL (RUGBY).

4 teams

FLYING MACHINES.

Including Models.

GOLF.

Individual Medal Competition.
Score Play.

30

Team Competition.
6 to play, 4 to count.

4 teams

GYMNASTICS.

A. Individual Competitions.

Voluntary Exercises.

20

1. Horizontal Bar, swinging movements
2. Horizontal Bar, slow movements.
3. Parallel Bars, slow and swinging movements.
4. Rings, steady.
5. Rings, flying.
6. Pommelled Horse, quick movements.
7. Rope Climbing.

Every competitor must take part in every item.

B. Team Competitions.

Voluntary Mass Exercises. The exercises may be those known as free gymnastics or exercises with hand apparatus.

1 team

Teams of not less than 16 nor more than 40.

C. Displays (Non-competitive).

HOCKEY.

3 teams

110

LACROSSE.

American Tournament System.   1 team

LAWN TENNIS.

Men's Singles.   12

Men's Doubles.   6 pairs

Ladies' Singles.   12

MOTOR BOATS.

Competition to be held on Southampton Water under the auspices of the Motor Yacht Club.

30 miles (48·27 kilometres) : round marked boats (as in the International Cup Race).

MOTOR RACING.

Races to be held on the Brooklands Racing Track at Weybridge.

1. **Flying Kilometre for Racing Cars** (1,093·6 yards).

2. About **9 miles** (14·4 kilometres) (3 times round the course) **Touring Car Races.** Cars to be not more than 30 h.p., and to carry 280 lbs. weight in addition to the driver and mechanic.

3. About **14 miles** (22·5 kilometres) (5 times round the course) **for Racing Cars** not exceeding 2,600 lbs. in weight, including driver and mechanic.

POLO.

Matches at Hurlingham under Hurlingham Club Rules.

	Maximum No. of Competitors from each Country
RIDING.	
Commemorative medals to all riders.	
RACQUETS.	
At Queen's Club, West Kensington.	**12**
Singles.	
Doubles.	**6 pairs**
ROWING.	
Eights (in best boats).	**2**
Fours ,,	**2**
Pairs ,,	**2**
Sculls ,,	**3 or 4?**
The Rowing events will take place on the 25th July, 1908, and the following days, under the management of the A.R.A., who are arranging that the Henley course shall be specially lengthened for this purpose.	
SHOOTING.	
I. RIFLE SHOOTING.	
Competitions at Bisley under the management of the National Rifle Association.	
Service Rifle of any country.	
Teams of 6.	
(*a*) At 500, 600, 900, and 1000 yards (457·2, 548·6, 823, and 914 metres).	**1 team**
(*b*) At 200 and 300 yards (183 and 274 metres).	**1 team**
Fifteen shots at each range.	
II. REVOLVER AND PISTOL SHOOTING.	**12**
III. RUNNING DEER SHOOTING.	**12**
Any rifle and position.	
IV. CLAY BIRD SHOOTING.	**12**

The Stadium will be capable of holding about 70,000 spectators, and will contain dressing-rooms, lavatories, and other accommodation for competitors in the Games.

The centre will be an arena of turf of oval shape, having a long axis of 700 feet and a short axis of 300 feet. Round this arena will be built two tracks, the inner for Running and the outer for Cycling. Running alongside the arena will be a huge swimming-bath, with a deep space in the middle for High Diving and Water Polo.

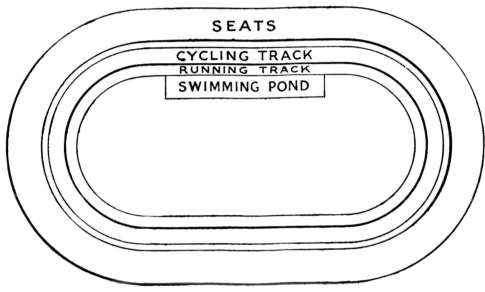

SEATS
CYCLING TRACK
RUNNING TRACK
SWIMMING POND

PLAN OF STADIUM.

Length of Turf, 235 yards (215·412 metres).

Length of Turf (exclusive of Lawn Tennis Courts), 136 yards 9 inches (124·584 metres).

Width of Turf, 99 yards 1 foot (90·797 metres).

Width of Turf (exclusive of Swimming Pond), 82 yards 2 feet (75·528 metres).

Running Track, 3 laps to 1 mile, 24 feet wide (7·315 metres). 1 lap = 586 yards 2 feet (536·375 metres).

Cycling Track, 2¾ laps to 1 mile, 35 feet wide (10·602 metres). 1 lap = 640 yards (585·199 metres).

Swimming Pond: length, 100 metres (109·363 yards). Width, 50 feet (15·172 metres). Depth at each end, 4 feet (1·188 metres). Depth in middle, 12 feet (3·658 metres).

Spottiswoode & Co. Ltd., Printers, New-street Square, London, E.C.

Lord Desborough and Pierre de Coubertin among the many dignitaries at the Inauguration of the Great Stadium on 26th May 1908.

American Triumphs at the Olympic Games

A RACE THAT BROKE TWO RECORDS

M. W. Sheppard, of the United States, won the 800 metres race at the Stadium in 1 min. 52 4-5 sec., beating the previous record by 3 1-5 sec. He went on for about five yards further, and also beat the British half-mile record in 1 min. 54 sec. Photograph by Illustrations Bureau.

A RECORD HIGH JUMP

H. F. Porter, of the United States, won the running high jump with an excellent leap of 6ft. 3in., which constitutes an Olympic record. Con Leahy, the Irishman, André, of France, and Somody, of Hungary, all tied at 6ft. 2in. Photograph by Halftones.

THE STRUGGLE FOR SUPREMACY	
BRITISH ISLES.	**UNITED STATES.**
Tug-of-War 1	Hammer Throwing 1
Swimming—400 metres 1	Running—1500 metres 1
„ 200 metres 1	„ 800 metres 1
Walking—3500 metres 1	Discus Throwing—Free Style 1
„ 10 miles 1	„ Greek Style 1
Running—Three Miles Team	Putting the Weight 1
Race 1	Standing Broad Jump 1
„ 3200 metres	Swimming—100 metres 1
Steeplechase .. 1	Wrestling—Catch-as-
„ Five Miles Flat .. 1	catch-can (Bantam).. 1
Cycling—660 Yards 1	Running High Jump 1
„ 20 kilometres 1	—
„ Team Pursuit Race 1	10
„ 5000 metres 1	The above figures were calcu-
„ 100 kilometres ... 1	lated up to Wednesday last, at
Archery—Ladies' National	which period the United King-
Round 1	dom had also scored 14 seconds
„ Men's York Round 1	against by the United States.
—	Sweden came a bad third with
15	only 3 wins.

Photograph]   A CROWD OF ENTHUSIASTIC AMERICANS IN ONE OF THE STANDS CHEERING THEIR COMPATRIOTS   *[Illustrations Bureau*

The United States team is the only one which has been pressing our own at all closely in the Olympic Games at the Stadium. At the time of writing the American athletes had had a series of successes, and on Tuesday last they won the only two finals decided, creating a fresh record in each case. The position on Wednesday was that as far as regards the Stadium events only Britain had won 15 to America's 10. Counting in the outside events, however, this country had the far larger preponderance of 30 wins to 14.

American Triumphs at the London Olympic Games 1908.

Four

THE 1908 LONDON OLYMPIC MARATHON

The marathon is today regarded not only as being a true examination of the limits of human endurance, a feat of both mental and physical stamina, but also as a popular symbol of community and harmony. Simply think of a marathon and images of streets packed with runners looking to better or test themselves, or to raise money for charities and good causes the world over, immediately spring to mind. Such streets are inevitably lined with crowds of well-wishers cheering for the participants, the spectrum of which runs from elite to absolute beginners. It was this spirit that was first invoked at the London Olympic Games of 1908, at which the marathon set the standard for what was to become the modern version of the event, and which also sparked controversy as well as generating mass appeal in almost equal measure.

The event was included in the first modern Olympics in Athens 1896, with its inspiration being based on the fabled epic undertaking of the Greek soldier Pheidippides who, acting as a messenger from the battlefield, ran without break from Marathon to Athens in 490BC.

Having delivered the message of Greek victory over the Persian army, it is said he collapsed and died. The organisers of the modern Olympics were keen to raise the marathon's profile, aware that such a dramatic sporting event which mercilessly examined the limits of human endurance could create mass appeal. It would, of course, also bring with it a ready-made ancient myth, a real sense of the history of athletic achievement that could immediately be associated with the revived modern Olympics.

The Amateur Athletic Association (AAA), established in 1880, was tasked with organising the Olympic versions of the regulation track and field events, but was unsure of how to come up with a suitable marathon route. The task was especially difficult given the fact that the length of the race was flexible at the time – the only agreement in place regarding a distance had been made at a meeting of the International Olympic Committee in The Hague in May 1907, where it was decided that the 1908 Olympics would include a marathon of around 25 miles, or 40 kilometres. Jack Andrew, a member of the AAA committee as well as honorary secretary of the

Pietro Dorando of Italy cheered on by thousands of spectators during the London 1908 Olympic Marathon.

116

Polytechnic Harriers, one of the country's first athletics clubs formed in 1883 and based in Chiswick in London, offered his club's services. It was soon agreed that he would oversee the planning of the marathon, and Andrew duly began organising the race with his running club, settling on a route beginning in Windsor's Great Park and finishing in Shepherd's Bush at the Great Stadium in White City. Plans detailing this route of roughly 25 miles were published in newspapers in November 1907. Whilst there was no formal requirement to begin and end in those places, Andrew felt this route captured the spirit and grandeur of the event and also preferred the point-to-point model of the Athens Olympic marathon, rather than a looped route beginning and ending in a stadium as used in Paris. He could not, however, have factored in or ultimately ignore the notable and powerful nature of royal influence and involvement, one which was key in the staging of the 1908 London Games overall.

The official trial marathon, held on the 25th of April 1908 and organised by the Polytechnic Harriers, set off at "The Long Walk", the magnificent avenue leading up to Windsor Castle in the grounds of Windsor Great Park, finishing at the running track at Wembley. It was planned that the runners simply continue for a further 5 miles for the actual Olympic marathon in July, finishing inside the Great Stadium and entering via the Royal Entrance. However, Andrew was later told that the official start for the Olympic event should be lengthened to be level with the castle's private East Terrace, near a bronze statue of Dako, Queen Victoria's favourite dog. This was given special permission by King Edward VII, with the official reason for this change being that it would ensure that the public could not interfere with the start, but it also conveniently allowed for a private view of proceedings for the Royal Family. Similarly, Andrew was advised that it would be fitting for the race to finish in sight of the Royal Box, adding an extra 385 yards which were to be run, unusually, in a clockwise direction to allow Queen Alexandra to have the best view possible. A further complication arose when organisers realised shortly before the Games began that the Royal Entrance wasn't suitable for the runners to use as planned - it was raised to allow easy access to carriages and simply did not open onto the track. An entrance diagonally opposite the Royal Box was therefore chosen instead and was accessed via a special path which was marked out to ensure the distance to the stadium remained at 26 miles. Another revision to the route was also required following protests over the fact that the final miles covered cobbles and tramlines, so the course was once more lengthened to cross the rough ground over Wormwood Scrubs, at one time one of London's main duelling grounds. Andrew and his team of planners were clearly kept busy throughout the planning process.

In distinct contrast to modern city marathons, the final route for the "great event", as it was described in the programme reproduced in this section, skirted around central London, crossing the Thames from the start in Windsor, moving through Eton and a series of market towns to the finish. It was more rural than urban and, with the revisions forced on Andrew put in place, the final total length for the race came to 26 miles

385 yards, or 42.195 kilometres. A detailed plan of the official route published exclusively for this book follows in this section. This distance was later approved as the official marathon standard in 1921 by the International Amateur Athletic Federation (IAAF) - Rule 240 of their Competition Rules - and has remained fixed as such to the present day. Urban transport development and the rebuilding of White City as the BBC headquarters have sadly removed all traces of the original 1908 route, save for a sole mile marker which can still be found on a house next to Barnes Bridge in Eton, reading "25 miles to go".

The 1908 London Olympic marathon was held on Friday 24th July 1908, with the start an interesting affair in and of itself as it featured a knot of Royal etiquette which had to be unpicked. The Crown Prince of Sweden was due to start the race, but protocol dictated he should defer to the Princess of Wales (later Queen Mary) who

Jack Andrews (middle) 1908 Olympic Marathon
Course Director

was also present, having been driven from her home at Frogmore on the far side of Great Windsor Park along with her children who were enthusiastic spectators. It was a potentially embarrassing situation. A plan was quickly put in place whereby the Princess of Wales pressed a button to relay a signal via electric cable from the East Terrace to a car at the starting line in which Lord Desborough sat. Upon receiving the signal he fired the starting pistol as the Crown Prince of Sweden shouted for the runners to begin.

Conditions were stifling and muggy as the 75 runners began at 2:30 pm. They were escorted by members of the Polytechnic Harriers Cycling Club with further support from motor vehicles, a rarity in sport at the time. The majority of the marathon passed largely without incident and was a disappointing one from a British sporting perspective. As the official 1908 reports show, 8 of the 12 entrants from the UK retired, a frantic opening pace of just over 5 minutes a mile set by British athletes Lord and Jack taking its toll along with the sweltering heat. The race did, however, clearly capture the public imagination, with a reported 250,000 people lining the route, with "all the aspect of the Thames on Boat Race day", as the official report states. Amateur sport had, for

Pietri Dorando (Italy)
First home in the marathon race, Windsor to the stadium.

the first time, generated mass appeal across society, with middle class competitors being cheered on by mostly working class spectators, watched in an official capacity by Lords and Royalty. However, the marathon was to go down in both Olympic and sporting history not just for this, but also due to the dramatic scenes at the end of the race as the runners entered the Great Stadium.

The Italian Dorando Petri (incorrectly identified by his first name in the programme), was comfortably ahead of the American Johnny Hayes in second, but was fading fast. Having initially begun his lap of the track in the wrong direction, drawing gasps of disbelief from the crowd, he collapsed, and was reportedly almost unconscious, in a scene no doubt echoing the classical myth of Pheidippides in the original marathon. The crowd was rapt as they watched Dorando being helped

to his feet, willing him to gather enough strength to cross the line, with Hayes closing in all the time. After collapsing again several times, the Italian eventually finished, staggering across the line with direct assistance from Jack Andrew, present in his capacity of Clerk of the Course, and another official as they supported him. This moment was captured in an iconic photograph appearing in this section which remains one of the most enduring images of the Olympic Games.

The London Games had been marked by some tension between the British and American teams. This rivalry stemmed from an incident at the opening ceremony where the American flag was flown at half mast, claimed later as an honest mistake, with the US flag bearer refusing to dip his country's standard in deference to the King in return. The differences were essentially cultural

118

at a time when accepted sporting demeanour was a new and fluid concept - the British felt the Americans could become brash competitors in their desire to win, with the US team feeling they were treated unfairly and were justified in their approach, seeing it as nothing more than nationalistic pride. It goes without saying that the marathon incident did little to ease the rivalry. Hayes was aghast that Dorando was initially announced as the winner despite the race marshals acting in clear contravention of the rules when they assisted the Italian. The American team immediately lodged a complaint which was eventually upheld, and Hayes was duly crowned with the Olympic gold medal as a result, his winning time recorded as 2 hours, 55 minutes and 18 seconds. His teammates victoriously carried him, clutching his trophy presented by the Greek Olympic Committee, aloft on a table in celebration.

Sir Arthur Conan Doyle, commissioned to write about the event for the Daily Mail, sat in the stands watching the drama unfold as Dorando was stripped of his title. He wrote that "The Italian's great performance can never be effaced from our records of sport, be the decision of the judges what it may." He also captured the mood of the crowd, one in awe of Dorando's performance, writing that "It is horrible, and yet fascinating, this struggle between a set purpose and an utterly exhausted frame." The official marathon record states that the officials feared he might die in the presence of the Queen – a prime example of unacceptable Edwardian etiquette as you're ever likely to come across - and that the Italian's heart had been displaced by more than half an inch, such was the demand of his physical labour. Queen Alexandra found him so deserving of recognition despite his disqualification that she presented him with a special silver-gilt trophy the following day once he had recovered sufficiently. Dorando was hailed as a sporting hero in the press, a trailblazing sports personality. Also impressed by his seemingly superhuman efforts, Conan Doyle later began a fund to raise money for the amateur athlete who, ironically, promptly turned professional, making a good living for several years through racing. Hayes followed suit with many others, with the two men staging rematches over the same distance of 26 miles 385 yards across the world.

The ongoing impact of the 1908 London marathon race cannot be underestimated. The sporting event was so significant and innovative as it was just that, the first true sporting event as we understand it now in modern terms. It led to worldwide marathon fever – an American spectator wrote an enthusiastic postcard home stating, in no uncertain terms, that he had "just seen the greatest race of the century." Sport suddenly had international significance. The marathon had a particular appeal that spanned class and age boundaries and led to the rise of the international sportsman celebrated in the popular press, as well as underlining the importance of impartial officials in future events, such was the potential rivalry between competing nations. The sheer human drama and widespread popularity of the marathon did at times threaten to steal the limelight from Coubertain's vision for the Olympics as a catalyst for peace and international understanding. However, the undeniable spirit instilled in all associated with the marathon event – athletes, spectators, society, entire nations - went on to characterise the Olympic movement, setting a new standard for modern sporting achievement.

JJ Hayes, official marathon winner back in New York training group of youths/children.

PIETRI DORANDO (ITALY)
FIRST HOME IN THE MARATHON RACE

J.J. HAYES (U.S.A)
WINNER OF THE MARATHON RACE

RUISLIP RESERVOIR

PARK WOOD

RUISLIP

13M.
20.92K.

BUCKINGHAM

IVER HEATH

UXBRIDGE

ICKENHAM

HILLINGDON

MIDDL

FROM BEACONFIELD

BLACK PARK

14m.
22.53K.

15M.
24.14K.

BACK LANE

16M.
25.74K.

18M.
28.96K.

17M.
27.35K.

WEXHAM

20M.
32.18K.

19M.
30.57K.

UXBRIDGE MOOR

TO LONDON

21M.
33.79K.

LANGLEY PARK

LANGLEY MARISH

IVER

UPON CUM CHALVEY

FROM MAIDENHEAD

22M.
35.4K.

23M.
37K.

SLOUGH

24M.
38.62K.

TO LONDON

25M.
40.23K.

WINDSOR CASTLE

THE PROPOSED STARTING POINT OF THE MARATHON
26 M. 41·84 K.

THE HOME PARK

STARTING POINT OF TRAIL RACE

B E R K S

WINDSOR CASTLE

ORGANISED BY

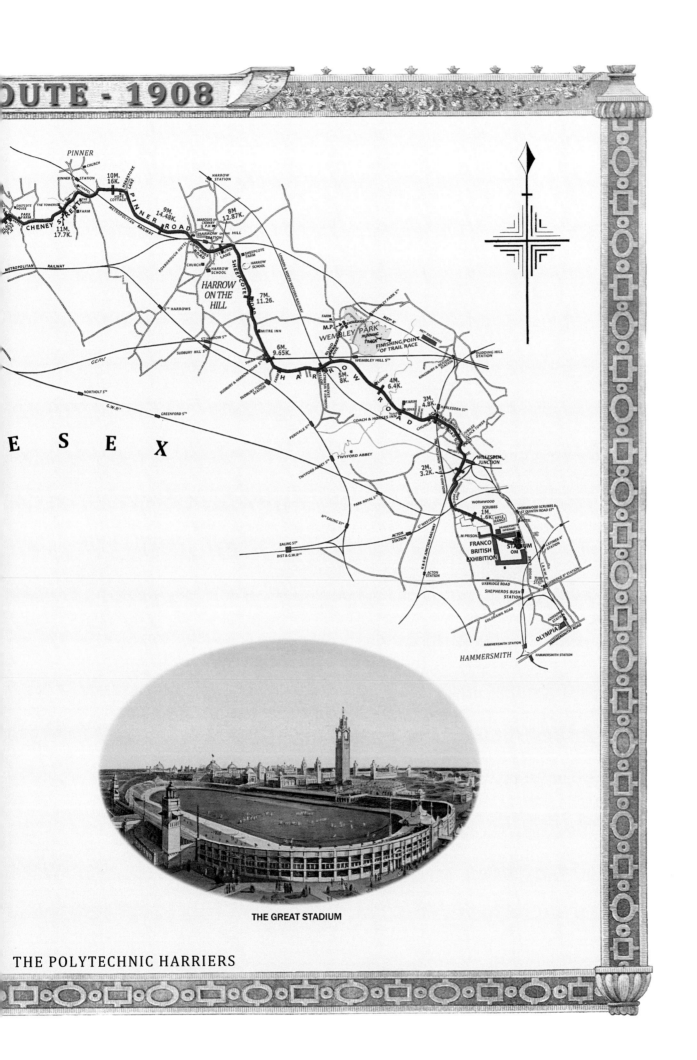

THE GREAT STADIUM

THE POLYTECHNIC HARRIERS

OLYMPIC GAMES, 1908.

Programme of

Marathon Race

— FROM —

WINDSOR CASTLE.

Windsor Castle

TO THE

Great Stadium,

Shepherd's Bush, W.

Friday, July 24th, 1908.

· · OFFICIALS · ·

Referee.
The RIGHT HON. LORD DESBOROUGH OF TAPLOW, C.V.O.

Judges.
Messrs. A. J. EGGLESTON, W. A. BROMMAGE, H. VENN, G. DUXFIELD, J. E. K. STUDD, and J. T. GREEN.

Timekeepers.
Messrs. W. M. BARNARD, C. J. PRATT and G. M. TODD,

Chief Clerk of the Course.
Mr. J. M. ANDREW.

Honorary Secretary.
Mr. P. L. FISHER.

Chief Marshals.
Messrs. E. BAMPFYLDE (Mayor of Windsor), R. MITCHELL and J. SULLIVAN.

Motor and Attendants Marshal.
Mr. I. B. DAVIDSON,

Medical Attendants and Examiners.
Dr. M. J. BULGER.   Dr. E. MOIR.
,, A. ROSCOE BADGER.   ,, T. H. E. MEGGS, and
,, J. SKEVINGTON.   Mr. F. MATTHEWS.

Clerks of the Course and Stewards.
Messrs. D. M. HOGG, L. H. HARRIS, J. F. DITCHMAN and B. DAVIES, assisted by members of the Polytechnic Harriers and Cyclists.

Baggage Stewards.
Messrs. W. FLINT, W. J. ANDREW, B. C. LONG, G. E. WALTER, G. S. DEARLING, and W. E. GURNEY.

Distance Table of Marathon Route.

Start Windsor Castle, East Terrace, 700 yards from Queen Victoria's Statue.

Miles.		Kilometres.	
1	=	1·6	Barnespool Bridge, Eton.
2	=	3·2	Windsor Road, about 50 yards past the " Prince of Wales " P.H.
3	=	4·8	Corner of High Street, Slough, and Uxbridge Road.
4	=	6·4	On road to Uxbridge.
5	=	8	Furze Lodge, on road to Uxbridge.
6	=	9·65	145 yards past " Crooked Billet " P.H.
7	=	11·26	Near Ivy Lodge, Iver Heath.
	=	12·87	Long Bridge, Uxbridge Moor.
	=	14·48	The Lodge, High Street, Uxbridge.
10	=	16	Near Uxbridge Common, on road to Ickenham.
11	=	17·7	On road to Ickenham.
12	=	19·3	On Bridge Approach at Ruislip and Ickenham Station, G. W. and G. C. Railways.
13	=	20·92	On Eastcote Road, near Ruislip School.
14	=	22·53	Near Eastcote post-office.
15	=	24·14	At Rummens Farm, near Pinner Gas Works.
16	=	25·74	On Pinner Road, opposite Penhurst Villa.
17	=	27·35	,, ,, 1, Hawthorne Villas.

Distance Table.—*continued.*

Miles.		Kilometres.	
18	=	**28·96**	Kenton Road, Harrow.
19	=	**30·57**	Near grounds of Harrow Nursery Co.
20	=	**32·18**	At Sudbury and Harrow Road Station, G. C. Railway.
21	=	**33·79**	At Wembley and Sudbury Station, L. & N. W. Railway.
22	=	**35·4**	Near sixth milestone at Stonebridge Park.
23	=	**37**	Midland Railway, Stonebridge Park, goods offices.
24*	=	**38·62**	No. 28, Railway Cottages, Willesden Junction.
25*	=	**40·23**	On Wormwood Scrubs.
26*	=	**41·84**	Entrance of Stadium, QQ. RR. SS.

26 miles **385** yards = **42·263** kilometres.   Full distance.

* A Rocket or Gun will be fired at these three points.

———

NOTE—-The metrical measurements are approximate.

———

NOTE.—The Distance Tablets have been arranged the reverse of the above, thus the 25th mile from the Stadium is at Barnespool Bridge, Eton.

A tape too far - Italian Dorando Pietri requiring a helping hand to cross the line first in the Marathon, 24th July 1908.

TIME TABLE, JULY 24th, 1908.

(APPROXIMATE.)

START		at	2.30	p.m.
SLOUGH	....	,,	2.47	,,
UXBRIDGE	....	,,	3.20	,,
RUISLIP	....	,,	3.50	,,
HARROW	....	,,	4.10	,,
WEMBLEY (L. & N.W.Rly.)		,,	4.30	,,
HARLESDEN (Clock Tower)		,,	4.45	,,
WORMWOOD SCRUBS		,,	4.54	,,
THE STADIUM	....	,,	5.5	,,

The Association beg to acknowledge with many thanks the following firms for their kindness in providing motor cars for the accommodation of officials :—S. F. Edge, Ltd. (Napier), The Car Supply Co., Ltd. (A. J. Pinto Leete), The Wolseley Co., Ltd. (E. H. Godbold), Mr. Ernest de Wilton, Mr. A. A. Mansell, Panhard Co., Ltd. (Mr. Ducros), Mr. H. A. Mears, and Mr. P. B. W. Tippetts.

The Association also acknowledge the valuable services of the Surveyors of the various Counties, Boroughs and Parishes traversed, and to the Metropolitan, Windsor and Bucks Police Forces for their invaluable help in the arrangements for this great event.

Instructions to Competitors

Last Train from Paddington for Competitors and Officials, 1.3 p.m.

The Race will be under the laws of the A.A.A.

The Association will arrange as far as possible for the convenience of competitors *en route*, but accept no responsibility, and competitors must therefore arrange with their own attendants to look after their requirements.

Costume.—The following A.A.A. Rule will be strictly enforced : —

> " Every Competitor must wear complete Clothing from the shoulder to the knees (*i.e.*, jersey sleeved to the elbows and loose drawers with slips). Any competitor will be excluded from taking part in the Race unless properly attired."

Competitors are requested to keep to the left side of the road.

Baggage.—Competitors must have their clothes packed in one bag and delivered to Baggage Car not later than **2** p.m. Each bag will be numbered and a check given to attendant of competitor. The check must be given to Baggage Attendant when bag is wanted, and it will then be dropped at the next hotel where arrangements have been made for dressing. A Special Car will follow to carry competitors who abandon the race. Dressing accommodation has been arranged at Great Western Railway, Windsor Station, where the authorities have kindly placed all the Waiting and Cloak Rooms at our disposal.

En Route.—Competitors and Attendants will find accommodation at the following hotels for a wash, etc. :—

Iver Heath, " The Crooked Billet."
Uxbridge, " Kings Arms Hotel."
Ruislip, " The Poplars."
    ,,   " The George Hotel."
Harrow, " Roxborongh Hotel."
Sudbury, " The Swan."

Refreshments *en route.*—The Oxo Company have been appointed Official Caterers and will supply the following free of charge to Competitors :—Oxo Athletes Flask, containing Oxo for immediate use. Oxo hot and cold; Oxo and Soda, Rice Pudding, Raisins, Bananas, Soda and Milk. Stimulants will be available in cases of collapse. Note—Eau de Cologne and sponges can be had for use of competitors from the Oxo representatives who will be stationed at the following positions on the route, where they will erect and manage refreshment booths :—

Ruislip, " The Poplars."
Harrow, " Railway Bridge."
Sudbury, " The Swan."
Harlesden, " Jubilee Clock Tower."

Dressing Arrangements at the Stadium in Room 28 for all Competitors.

Windsor Castle.

130

ENTRIES.

					TIME.			Position at Finish.
					H.	M.	S.	
1	LYNCH, J. M.	...	... Australasia	...				
2	AITKEN, W. V.	...	... ,,	...				
3	BLAKE, G. B.	...	... ,,	...				
4	BAKER, J. M.	...	... South Africa	...				
5	MOLE, A. B.	...	... ,,	...				
6	STEVENS, C. E.	...	... ,,	...				
7	VINCENT,	...	... ,,	...				
8	HEFFERON, C.	...	... ,,	...				
9	COULCUMBERDOS, G.	... Greece	...	...				
10	COUTOULAKIE, A.	... ,,	...	...				
11	NIEMINEN	...	... Finland	...	...			
12	LIND, G.	...	... Russia	...	...			
13	BRAAMS, W. T.	...	... Holland	...	...			
14	VOSBERGEN, A. C. H.	... ,,	...	...				
15	WAKKER, W. W.	... ,,	...	...				
16	THEUNISSEN, W. F.	... ,	...	...				
17	BUFF, G. J. M.	...	... ,,	...	...			
18	CELIS, F.	...	... Belgium	...	...			
19	DORANDO, P.	...	... Italy	...	...			
20	BLASI, U.	...	... ,,	...	...			
21	BLASI, U.	...	... ,,	...	...			
22	COCCA, A.	...	... ,,	...	...			
23	DURANDO, P.	...	... ,,	...	...			
24	FORSHAW, J.	...	... U.S.A.	...	...			
25	HATCH, S. H.	...	... ,,	...	...			
26	HAYES, J. J.	...	... ,,	...	...			
27	LEE. J. J.	...	... ,,	...	...			

			TIME.			Position at Finish.
			H.	M.	S.	
28	LORZ, F.	... ... U.S.A.				
29	MORRISSEY, T. P.	... ,, ...				
30	O'MARA, W.	... ... ,, ...				
31	RYAN, M. J.	... ... ,, ...				
32	THIBEAU, A,	... ... ,, ...				
33	TEWANINA, L. ...	... ,, ...				
34	WELTON, A. R....	... ,, ...				
35	WOOD, W.	... ... ,, ...				
36	MULLER, H.	... ... Germany				
37	REISER, F.	... ... ,, ...				
38	NETTLEBECK, P.	... ,, ...				
39	TORNROS, G.	... ... Sweden				
40	SVANBERG, J. F.	... ,, ...				
41	PETERSSON, J. G.	... ,, ...				
42	LANDQUIST, S. L.	... ,, ...				
43	LINDQVIST, J. ...	... ,, ...				
44	BERGVALL, J. T.	... ,, ...				
45	LUNDBERG, J. G. A.	... ,, ...				
46	RATH, E.	... ... Austria				
47	KWIETON, F. ...	... ,, ...				
48	NOJEDKY	... ... Bohemia				
49	HANSEN, R. C. ...	... Denmark				
50	JORGENSEN, J. F.	... ,, ...				
51	MERENYI, L.	... ... Hungary				
52	DUNCAN, A.	... ... Gt. Britain & Ireland				
53	BEALE, J. G.	... ... ,, ,,				
54	LORD, T.	... ... ,, ,,				
55	PRICE, J.	... ... ,, ,,				

9469 B   PIETRI DORANDO (ITALY)   ROTARY PHOTO, E.C
FIRST HOME IN THE MARATHON RACE, WINDSOR TO THE STADIUM,
RECEIVING THE GOLD CUP FROM H.M. QUEEN ALEXANDRA.

ENTRIES—*continued*.

				TIME.			Position at Finish.
				H.	M.	S.	
56	BARRETT, H. F.	... Gt. Britain & Ireland					
57	THOMPSON, F. B.	... ,,	,,				
58	BARNES, E.	... ,,	,,				
59	WYATT, A.	. . ,,	,,				
60	APPLEBY, F.	... ,,	,,				
61	JACK, T.	... ,,	,,				
62	STEVENSON, S.	... ,,	,,				
63	CLARKE. W. T.	... ,,	,,				
64	SIMPSON, F.	... Canada ...	...				
65	LAWSON, H.	... ,, ...	...				
66	GOLDSBORO, W.	... ,, ...	...				
67	GOULDING, G. ...	... ,, ...	...				
68	WOOD, W.	... ,, ...	...				
69	COTTER, E.	... ,, ...	...				
70	NOSEWORTHY, F.	... ,, ...	...				
71	CAFFERY, J.	... ,, ...	...				
72	LONGBOAT, T. ...	... ,, ..	...				
73	LISTER, G.	... ,, ...	...				
74	BURN, A.	... ,, ...	...				
75	TAIT, J....	... ,, ...	...				

Railway Arrangements.

The G.W. Railway Special Train for Competitors and friends will leave Paddington at 1.3 p.m., arriving at Windsor 1.27.

Rules of Marathon Race.

1. The Marathon race of about 40 kilometres will be run on a course marked out on public roads by the Amateur Athletic Association and will finish on the running track in the Stadium, where part of 1 Lap will be run.

2 Each competitor must send with his entry a medical certificate of fitness to take part in the race, and must further undergo a medical examination previous to the start by the medical officer or officers appointed by the British Olympic Council.

3. A competitor must at once retire from the race if ordered to do so by a member of the medical staff appointed by the British Olympic Council to patrol the course.

4. No competitor either at the start or during the progress of the race may take or receive any drug. The breach of this rule will operate as an absolute disqualification.

5. The station of each competitor at the start will be determined by lot, and in the event of the competitors being too numerous to be started on a single line, they will be started on two or more lines.

6. Each competitor shall be allowed two attendants, who shall wear on breast and back the same distinctive number as the competitor.

7. The attendants shall during the progress of the race remain behind the competitor they are attending or be sufficiently in front to prevent them giving pacing assistance. Non-observance of this rule will disqualify the competitor.

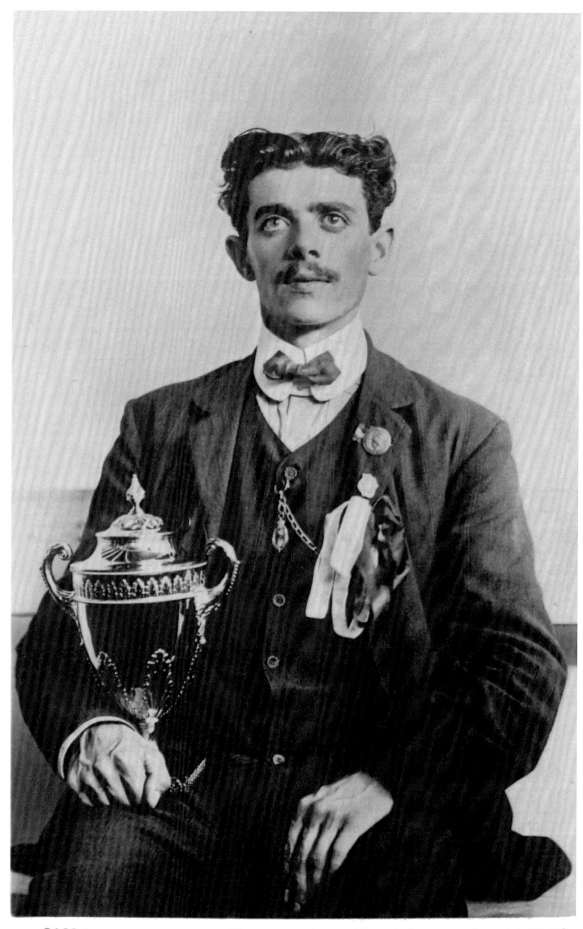

9469 A PIETRI DORANDO (ITALY) ROTARY PHOTO, E.C.
FIRST HOME IN THE MARATHON RACE, WINDSOR TO THE STADIUM.
WITH THE QUEEN'S CUP.

8. Attendants will not be permitted to see the start of the contest, but must proceed in a body from the Attendants' Assembly Hall at Windsor to the appointed place 5 miles (8 kilometres) from the start and join their competitors as they pass. Upon arrival at the Stadium the attendants must leave the competitors and enter at a different gate. No attendant will be allowed on the track.

9. Any competitor whose attendant or attendants obstruct another competitor will be disqualified.

10. Each competitor must provide his own attendants and required refreshments.

11. When a competitor retires from the race, his attendants must also leave the route.

TROPHY PRESENTED BY THE GREEK OLYMPIC COMMITTEE.

Description of Route.

The race starts from Windsor Castle, near East Terrace (700 yards from Queen Victoria's Statue), through Thames Street, across Thames Bridge into High Street Eton, past Eton College and Playing Fields, along Windsor Road until High Street, Slough, is reached. Road towards London for 925 yards, then turn to the left into Uxbridge Road, over Great Western Railway, through George Green (Green Man P.H. 4½ miles), keep Langley Park on right and continue straight road to Long Bridge (River Colne). After crossing this keep to the left, cross Canal into New Windsor Street, here turn to the left for a few yards and then to the right into Windsor Street, here turn to the left and keeping Parish Church on the left you enter High Street, Uxbridge. Here turn to the right towards London for about 500 yards, turning to the left at Sign Post for Ickenham, crossing Uxbridge Common and keep to the right until Ickenham Village is reached, here turn to the left, crossing Great Western and Great Central Railways (Ruislip and Ickenham Station) for Ruislip. Keeping "The Poplars" on the right you enter Ruislip Village. Take Eastcote Road (opposite "George Hotel") and keep to the right of this and take first turning to right after passing Eastcote Post Office. Three hundred yards past Pinner Gas Works turn sharp to the right, cross Metropolitan Railway, and keep to the right until "Roxborough Hotel," Harrow, is reached. Here you re-cross the Metropolitan Railway into Lowlands Road. Run parallel with the railway until Sheepcote Lane is reached; there turn to the right, and passing the "Mitre Hotel" on the

9468 A   J. J. HAYES (U.S.A.)   ROTARY PHOTO. E.C.
WINNER OF THE MARATHON RACE,
WINDSOR TO THE STADIUM.
BEING CARRIED ON TABLE WITH TROPHY.

left you reach the Harrow Road at Sudbury. Here keep to the left until Sudbury Station, L. & N. W. Railway is reached.

From here follow tram lines until the Jubilee Clock Tower at Harlesden. Here turn to the right through Station Road, across L. & N. W. Railway at Willesden Junction Station, past Railway Cottages. Take first turning to the left into Old Oak Lane. After passing under the Great Western Railway lines, turn sharp to the left across Old Oak Common and Wormwood Scrubs, keeping the footpath between the Prison and Hammersmith Infirmary into Ducane Road for Exhibition Grounds, where a special entrance will be made and a course roped for competitors to QQ. RR. SS. entrance to Stadium.

All vehicular traffic will have to leave competitors at the Clock Tower, Harlesden, and go through High Street to the College Park Hotel, turn to the right here for the Stadium, and enter No. 4 Gate in Wood Lane.

9468 B   J. J. HAYES (U.S A)   ROTARY PHOTO. E C.
WINNER OF THE MARATHON RACE.
WINDSOR TO THE STADIUM.

OLYMPIC GAMES LONDON - 1908

ENTRANCE TO THE GREAT STADIUM

International  Olympiad.

OLYMPIC GAMES
OF
LONDON 1908.

ARENA TICKET.

This is to certify that

W. M. Barnard

is an official representing the [1]

_a.a.a._

and is entitled to pass into the Arena on

MONDAY, July [2] _25th 1908_

between the hours of [3] _2.30pm_

Signed [4] _P. L. Fisher_

For the British Olympic Council,

Robert S. de C. Laffan

Hon Sec

(1) Here insert the name of the Association represented.
(2) Here insert the date.
(3) Here insert the hours.
(4) The Secretary or other authorised representative of the Association to sign here.

PICTURE CREDITS
AND DEDICATIONS

Lord Desborough, Founding President of the British Olympic Association.

MAPS, PLAN AND SURVEYS

Street Maps from Bartholomew's Pocket Atlas and Guide to London 1908.

Courtesy of Collins Bartholomew Ltd. www.bartholomewmaps.com

Plan of the Route of the 1908 London Olympic Marathon ©*Mapseeker Publishing Ltd.*

Original archive courtesy of University of Westminster Archive Services.

Memorabilia, Images and Photographs 1908 Olympic Games

Pages 1, 7, 87-89, 90, 91, 93-113, 116, 118, 122-125, 127-129, 131-141, 143, 145.

© Special Collections - Academic Services – The University of Birmingham (**William Barnard Collection**)

Pages 2, 6, 9, 36, 40, 42, 44, 115, 119, 130, 142 © *Mapseeker Publishing Ltd.*

Pages 10, 13, 17, 21, 25, 29, 33, 92, 126 © *GettyImages Ltd.*

Pages 117, 146 © *University of Westminster Archive Services*

Pages 5, 84 © *Museum of London*

Pages 85, 86 © *Wenlock Olympian Society*

Additional views and vistas with special thanks to Berian Williams Antique maps and Prints, Ash Rare Prints, and Steve Bartrick Antique Maps and Prints.

www.antique-prints-maps.co.uk www.ashrare.com www.antiqueprints.com

The commemorative print of the Route of the London 1908 Marathon is available at *www.mapseeker.co.uk*

July 21.st
1908.

Dear Sir,

In sending you a formal
receipt for the donation you were
so good as to send in response to
the appeal on behalf of the British
Olympic Council to enable us to
carry out the Olympic Games in a
suitable manner, I take the opportunity
of expressing our grateful thanks
for your most kind assistance. The appeal
as you probably know has been answered
in the most generous manner by all
classes of our countrymen, and has resulted
in a sum which will allow us to do full
justice to the occasion.
With renewed thanks I remain yours truly
Desborough.

DEDICATION TO WILLIAM BARNARD

William Murrell Barnard held the twin distinctions of being senior timekeeper at the London Olympics of 1908 and the executive officer of the Amateur Athletics Association (AAA). As such, he was implicitly involved in overseeing the rise of amateur sports - a movement to which he devoted his life - to unprecedented heights during the early 20th century, safeguarding its popularity and growth for over 40 years. William would hold the prestigious position of Treasurer of the AAA for a period of almost 22 years and was later honoured as a Life Vice President of the AAA. His zeal for amateur sport culminated in the defeat of a motion to allow professional athletes to enter the Olympics at a meeting of the Olympic Federation in Berlin in 1930, a victory attributed to his impassioned speaking.

An adept sprinter in his younger years, he joined the Polytechnic Harriers Athletics Club in 1884 and went on to hold the office of club treasurer for a period of 25 years.

A keen businessman with a sharp mind – an accountant by trade for his 56 year working life - he not only kept time but also organised amateur athletics meetings at Wembley Park for his club, often attracting gates of around 30,000 people during the halcyon days of amateur sport following the 1908 Games.

It is hoped that this book be a fitting tribute to an individual who is often overlooked in Olympic history, but who nonetheless devoted so much of his time, notable abilities and boundless energy to ultimately contribute, alongside more widely recognised distinguished sporting visionaries, to setting the Games on the road to its present worldwide popularity.

The original archive from the 1908 London Olympic Games laid out in a simple scrapbook of mementoes by William Barnard presented in this book are still preserved in the Archives of Birmingham University.

William Murrell Barnard